All War and Welsh Cakes

All War and Welsh Cakes

Ros Gudgeon

Memory Lane

First published in Great Britain by Memory Lane
ISBN 978-0-9567697-1-8
Printed and bound by Good News, Ongar, England.

To all my family, past, present and future.

CONTENTS

Finders Keepers

It lay warm, fresh and gently steaming in the road. I couldn't believe my luck. It was early morning and the milkman's horse had just passed leaving this bonus all for me. The day had not lost its stillness yet, there was no one else at all to be seen and not a curtain twitched. I just had to run home and back with a bucket and shovel, before anyone else spotted the treasure.

This was wartime, and we were all 'digging for victory', aiming to produce sufficient fruits and vegetables to bring about Hitler's downfall. Since all the waste skins, peelings and rare food scraps were regularly collected by 'Tommy the Wash' to turn into pigswill for the same ultimate aim, manure was about the only readily available fertiliser, and was priceless beyond pearls. If only I could fill my bucket quickly, my standing would be high enough for me to get away with murder for possibly two days – or more even!

I should have spent less time basking in anticipated promises; before I could drag our biggest (and heaviest) bucket back along the street, my prize was gone, and the big boys from further down the street were leaning against their front windowsill looking smug. I could only fix them a withering glare.

I couldn't give up now. I wondered if Margaret was about yet. Margaret was my best friend that week, and lived in the house at the corner, about six doors away from mine. There were four of us altogether; Margaret, known as Mar, Kathleen (Kaff to us), Joan from the next street and myself. We usually met up together on the way to school, were in the same class and always played together. There was a constant subtle shifting of degrees of loyalty which only served to make one a 'best' friend one week, another the next.

Mar was always game for adventure and risk. She was the smallest of our group, though in seniority of age was succeeded only by Kaff. Her mother was a widow, and Mar only knew her father as the man in the large faded sepia photograph hanging above the fireplace. Mar's mother had always worked to provide for them both, and, though there seemed to be an abundance of supportive aunties, Mar was tough and independent. She might look quite delicate and elf like, with a dark wing of hair over a pale complexion, but Mar had a core of iron. When we squabbled, her pale blue eyes were like ice daggers.

Mar was enthusiastic about going across the field to look for horse manure, and was quickly geared up with bucket and shovel. She was as aware as I was of the caché that a bucket of manure offered, so we clanked off happily together.

Our street was actually circular, a short road on two sides neatly bisecting the circumference of a circular access road leaving the centre lush with meadow grass, but Mar and I ignored this area where wild mountain ponies sometimes wandered in to forage. With the wisdom and experience of a childhood in wartime, we could be sure that any manure from this source would be spotted and collected almost before it hit the ground, so we left the circle of houses, passing the allotments at the back to head for the field beyond. This simple expedition carried the thrill of forbidden territory, a place where I was not allowed to go on my own. The field itself was enormous. As we stood at the kissing gate entrance, the distant hedge on the far side marked the edge of my world, with only the remote tips of the hills in the next valley showing as dark shadows above it. At the other side, iron railings bordered the road which fell away to the town in our valley. Between them, the rolling contours of dips and hillocks and a variety of grasses provided grazing for sheep, horses and cows at varying times. When it rained, there was even a pond at the bottom end which drained very slowly, often over a period of weeks, into a corner ditch. With the climate of the Welsh Valleys it was a novelty to find the bottom of the field dry at all!

Our luck was riding high; horses had been let into the field that day and we quickly filled our buckets. Not only that, but a recce along the far hedge yielded a couple of broken branches for the firewood store.

The presentation of my spoils was not a complete success however. Mam pointed out rather sharply that while manure might be good for the garden, the same could not be said for my shoes and socks, and the gift of firewood was received with a patient sigh as the tear in my dress was revealed.

By the end of the weekend all was forgotten, as we covered some of the same ground on our Sunday family outing – a walk with Mam and Dad both carefully dressed and polished, and me in my 'second best' outfit.

Dad held his arm uncomfortably across his chest, and Mam hung on to it. I loved to run on by myself across the fields, eager to find treasures in the long grasses, like the stalks with their 'shivery shake' heads which did just that but more vigorously than any other. I gave no thought to the seasons of berries and fruits, but dashed about excitedly wondering which I would find; if not tiny wild strawberries, then perhaps raspberries, wimberries or blackberries. I was deaf to the little arrows aimed at my bubble of excitement.

'Keep on the path. Mind you don't step in anything. Don't get dirty. Don't slide down those banks – your knickers will get all green.'

Now I was at the end of the path that marked the public right of way across the golf links. A broad sweep on the right, along the shoulder of the hill, marked the lines of the golf course, separated from our pathway by a border guard of sheep endlessly patrolling and cropping a swathe of no man's land.

The drop of the hill down to the stream was so tempting. Mam and Dad, of course, would turn left following the contour of the land till they reached a stile to the lane. Deaf to Mam's entreaties to 'come and walk tidy' I launched myself down the bank, gathering momentum over the fine downland grass. Feeling slightly guilty, I compromised by deciding that even if there were no raspberries to be found beside the stream, then I wouldn't go looking for watercress. Mam only sighed when I caught up with them, empty handed.

Then I saw the hens loose in the lane, and I was off. Sure enough, a search along the hedgerow yielded two eggs, a whole week's ration for one person in those days! Mam and Dad stood and deliberated. At first they wanted nothing to do with what might be construed as stolen goods, but upon reflection, the lane was a public highway, not part of the farm, so the eggs might be considered a treasure trove. I proudly carried them home in triumph and Mam boiled one for my tea. But it was bad, so she threw the other one away too.

It's hardly surprising that Mam was a bit wary of my 'special find.' Her most surprising find had occurred the week before.

The Blitz bombing had begun and continued relentlessly. We heard about it on the radio, read about it, discussed it in low tones as part of the general anxiety and fear of the war years, but it was all taking place far away from our quiet valley. Even when Cardiff and Newport were bombed and we watched the flickering glow in the sky as fires burned, we still felt somehow oddly protected by the range of twisting hills between us. We carried on with the habits of our gentle lives, and only the weather could put a stop to our weekend family stroll.

The day of Mam's 'special find' we were returning from a pleasant walk, on a sunny day, anticipating the pleasure of a 'dripping slice' with a cup of tea. But as we turned the last corner, all thoughts of dripping, with its lovely brown jelly, fled!

Our small front lawn, our patch of green gentility which had not been sacrificed to Hitler's downfall, was occupied. There were bundles and suitcases strewn across the precious grass and two weary young women sitting on the front doorstep. They introduced themselves. They were to be our evacuees who'd been bombed out of Dover and they had come to stay with us 'for the duration.' As soon as I heard that phrase, I knew they'd been staying a long time. 'For the duration' was the stock answer to any of my questions which began with 'How long will it be till…?' or 'When will…?' I didn't know that the phrase had been picked up from the government's statements on measures taken in the light of wartime events, trying to combine the burying of bad news with a little hope and sweetness. I only knew it meant 'almost forever.'

Mam's reaction to our sudden guests ran two ways – two more ration books brought more food into the house, but they also came with two more mouths to feed.

With no washing machine, and water heated via the living room fire (controlled by coal rationing), Mam's time seemed to be fully taken up with keeping the house and all its inhabitants clean and fed. She had heard that some housewives had taken to using place mats on the table instead of tablecloths, but Mam would have no truck with such laziness. No meal in our house would ever be found wanting for a clean tablecloth. Just because there was a war on, it was no excuse for not looking tidy and living tidy.

It was some comfort that our evacuees were not big eaters and often passed their unwanted sweet ration over to Mam. But no doubt she did pay for it in labour. The phrase had not been coined in those days, but it was in those early years of my life that I learned 'there is no such thing as a free lunch'.

The Need of Gifts

It was one of those days when I didn't mind so much that all the weekly sweet ration had been used up. In theory, when we went shopping on Saturday, we used all our sweet coupons on one glorious buying binge and then practised self-rationing through the week. In reality we were usually sweetless before Wednesday.

However, there were times when this was an easier hardship. Such was the time when the runner beans were long and lushly green on the stalk and my idea of heaven was a plate heaped with the tender juicy pods, a tiny knob of butter on the top slowly softening to a golden trickle. In our garden, beans were abundant; it was only the meagre weekly ration of butter which presented a problem – but so small a problem as to be none at all.

Mam came out of the larder with a glint in her eye.

'How would you like gooseberry tart for Sunday dinner?' she asked, brandishing a lump of lard. Fantastic! We seemed to have been suffering from a monotony of rice pudding lately, and it was a dish that seemed to elude Mam's culinary skill; it was either so watery and gritty that it ran off the plate, or so solid that it even resisted slicing.

I knew we didn't have gooseberries in the garden, but if Mam had decided that we would have gooseberry tart, then gooseberry tart there would be. We wouldn't be buying the gooseberries from Jones the Fruit either. He was hard put to find a few weary apples and pears to put out for sale. Exotica such as gooseberries, raspberries and strawberries were grown in back gardens, picked and consumed virtually on the spot, the flavour and sweetness all the more delicious for being a food that was unrestricted and plentiful. I was puzzled though; our gooseberry crop had failed that year, so how would Mam made a tart?

Now for Mam's magic bit – turning a lump of lard into a gooseberry tart. She went down the garden path at an eager trot, with the air of one who has worked out the battle plan in every detail and is now beginning the military manoeuvres.

Minutes later I was called to run an errand. Mam was wrapping a bundle of rhubarb in newspaper, lots of it, so much that the resulting parcel looked more like a shrouded dead cat.

'Take this to Mrs Smith the Corner. Tell her fresh pulled it is, and we've got plenty.'

This was odd. I knew Mam didn't like Mrs Smith ('give herself airs and graces that one'), and Mam had just pulled every stick of rhubarb to be had in the garden. I hoped Mrs Smith wouldn't think I'd taken her a dead cat.

I need not have worried. Mrs Smith left me standing on the doorstep while, with a long bony forefinger, she drilled an exploratory hole in the parcel.

'Rhubarb!' she said, her lips so tight that her face looked like a squeezed lemon. 'Take a lot of sugar that.' Even her tone was sour. It was as if she had received a message in a secret code (as indeed she had), and wished she was unable to understand it. She swept off to her larder, brisk and tight lipped, emerging to thrust a paper bag at me. Not a newspaper wrapper-upper, Mrs Smith; much too genteel.

Of course I had to explore the contents before I handed the bag to Mam, her tart-plate at the ready. Potatoes. Mam was not best pleased. Potatoes we had a-plenty.

That morning I seemed to spend a week going between various neighbours with bag or bundle; taking potatoes, bringing back onions, taking lettuce, bringing back a magazine. But gooseberries never featured. Only once did I return empty handed, but with a cryptic message that 'Bill would be round after dark.' Huh! I wasn't a stupid kid. I knew that miners had a far more generous ration of coal than the rest of us, and some of the extra often went into the barter system. So I knew that, come nightfall, a bucket of coal would be delivered discreetly to our back door.

By this time, I'd quite gone off the idea of gooseberry tart, and even Mam's enthusiasm was flagging. Then aunty Win called.

We hadn't had a visit from aunty Win in months. She lived higher up in the next valley, a distance which involved quite a long and complicated bus journey, going down one valley, crossing over to the next and then winding upwards again. Usually all the aunts would meet together only on Sunday visits to Gran's house, well up along the mountain road, overlooking three valleys.

Aunty Win sat back, enjoying her cup of tea and Mam's mounting anticipation of the customary 'hospitality gift.' When the social niceties could be stretched no further and she judged the tension more than satisfying, aunty Win pulled open her weighty frail with a flourish.

'Lovely early gooseberries we've got.'

She stated what was plainly obvious.

'I would have made jam, see, but the sugar wouldn't go to it.'

She paused on an expectant note. It was Mam's turn now.

I think, just for a moment, I was slightly ahead of Mam here. We'd stripped the garden of just about everything except potatoes in order to end up with no gooseberries, and now we had gooseberries galore and nothing to offer in acceptance of the prize.

But Mam wasn't thrown for long. First the casual, tinkly laugh, then, 'Oh, I been saving sugar, hoping to make some jam. I'll bring some over when I come.'

At a stroke she'd saved the situation and given herself a breathing space, though I had no doubt that I'd be doing the breathing – jogging around the neighbours again, launched at the ones likely to come up with sugar as a return gift now that Mam was stuck with making gooseberry jam as well as tart.

I have since tried to work out how this system came to be, but I don't think reason comes into it. It was structured for a time and a place, when and where people were not only poor, but rationed and restricted in every facet of daily life.

To be able to give was synonymous with another life, with wealth, abundance and security; to ask for anything was both an admission of poverty and an inability to cope, so it was a matter of pride never to ask. Thus the coded rhubarb and potatoes and lettuces carried the system. Couple this concept with a natural generosity of spirit which existed in those South Wales Valleys then, and you turned the whole thing on its head. If in need, don't ask – present gifts.

Take Away Food

Rationing, to me, was the natural order of things. Nothing ever went stale, and there was rarely anything left over at the end of the week – quite the contrary in fact.

Shopping was uncomplicated too. Everyone was registered with one grocer of their choice, and one butcher, which cut out all the 'shopping around' of present day living. The difficult bit was working out how to stretch the meagre amounts to last the week.

Every Tuesday, Mam took her weekly grocery order (plus ration books) to the grocer and took delivery every Thursday. I once asked why she never put any quantities on the list, just 'butter, sugar, tea, cheese' etc. Mam shrugged.

'No point,' she said. 'If it's on ration we get our allowance, and if it's not we get what Mr Pegler can spare – if he's got any.'

Seasons had much significance since everyone grew as much food as they could, and the age of refrigeration was yet to come. Strange to think that I had never been in a house that had a fridge until I was grown up and beginning my career in teaching.

Just as our childhood games followed a set pattern every year – hec (hopscotch), whip-and-top, tag, skipping – so we went along with the seasons that gave us the first spring shoots of rhubarb and early potatoes, through a variety of fruit and vegetables, to winter cabbage.

I was also in the fortunate position of having two sets of grandparents who kept chickens, so our menus were less limited by the rule of two eggs per person per week per ration book. During our regular once weekly (at least) visits to one or other of the grandparents, there was always 'a little something to take home and mind how you squeeze it,' carefully and discreetly handed over, wrapped and disguised in twists of newspaper. At the end of the war, the firing ceased but rationing went on for some time.

1947 was a severe winter. It arrived, quite suddenly, one evening in December. Till then, winter was never the way I imagined or wanted it to be. It was usually a period of relentless icy rain driven by a spiteful wind which lashed out sharply at every corner and hilltop. What I longed for was a winter the way I saw it in my comics.

I always felt a thrill of anticipation when, at some point in November, my weekly comic arrived with the title heading embellished with decorative blobs of snow, and sprigs of holly etched in the corners of the front page. The characters in the stories, in their cute woolly caps and mittens, always had fun tobogganing, skating and skiing. The nearest I ever got to this was sliding along the pavement when the rain gave way to a hard frost. My woolly hat and mittens quickly became icily soggy, and Wellington boots did not provide adequate insulation against rain whipped to a chill by the wind. For me, it was a time to stay indoors and hug the fire for its meagre, rationed warmth. The afternoon and early evening were the best times in winter. Then I could go to play at a friend's house or have a friend to visit, and the front room was opened. The very fact of being in the front room imposed its own discipline of playing sedately for fear of creasing the cushions, rumpling the hearth rug or otherwise disturbing its cherished but rigid formality. A rubber of 'Snakes and Ladders' or 'Ludo' was about as rowdy as front room boisterous play could get. As was common practice at the time, the front room was principally reserved for Christmas day, for the infrequent visits of distant relatives, and for when the vicar called.

When the snow came that year, I was playing up at Margaret's house, six doors away. There, the curtains were drawn against an early dusk and quickly deepening dark, and there was a fire in the front room.

It seemed no time at all until Dad was knocking at the door, come to take me home. I was all ready to protest until I glimpsed what was happening outside.

The street light next to Margaret's house was still a post-war novelty, and its glow highlighted what seemed to be a feather bed bursting from its covers. Grey houses with their curtain blanked windows and darker grey roofs, normally all blurred together into vague shadows and outlines after dark, were gone. I gazed at a different world of sharp white shapes, dazzling and glinting where the street lights struck them. It was the pages of *Dandy* and *Beano* come to life. Now I too could enjoy the same antics of my comic characters. This was serious snow, nothing like the occasional slushy inch or two of my past experiences.

Home was barely an hundred yards away, yet we battled through blinding snow whipping down from the mountains and beginning to build up into drifts that were already knee deep. With Dad to hang on to so that I didn't get blown away, it was exhilarating.

I could barely sleep for excitement that night, and woke to an unfamiliar silent stillness, the world I knew buried in a whiteness which began at the bedroom window and sloped away beyond where the hedge had been yesterday, like an excess of frothy cream over a pudding.

There followed days of glorious chaos; no school, odd meals at odd times, and hours of newly invented games, most of which involved sliding down snow on whatever objects were at hand – tin trays, bits of old prams, padded backsides…

Sundays always followed the same pattern. In the morning we went to church, and afterwards called at Grandad's house, which lay halfway up the hill from town and so provided a convenient break on the climb home. Fortified by a good dinner, we then took to the upward road again to Gran's house, a mile and a half away. It therefore seemed quite logical to refer to each house as either going 'up top' or 'down below,' and although morning service took place between the two visits, I'm sure the references had no theological significance.

Mam was determined that 'a bit of snow' would not prevent the Sunday visit to Gran's, in spite of further falls overnight. Since I could not be left in the house alone, and Dad would not allow Mam to make the journey by herself, we all set off together, straight after Sunday dinner.

A wide passageway had been cut through the snow where there were houses, but as the road turned towards the mountain and the streets petered out, so the snow banks fell away until the road surface re-appeared, glassy and frosted. I was quite disappointed.

Then the road turned again and began a steep rise up the hillside. Each turn brought ever-increasing levels of snow. Soft at first and ankle deep, it suddenly became a high white wall covering every landmark – hedges, trees, bushes and rocks.

Dad urged common sense and advised turning back, but there was no stopping Mam.

'I been up and down this road all through the blackout. Snow won't hurt.' I was with Mam – this was even better than my comics.

Up we went, where we thought the grassy bank and the hedge might be. It was like standing on the shoulders of the world, with only the tops of the telegraph poles to guide us. Dad insisted we worked our way from pole to pole, so that if the snow gave way the top of the hedge would be not too far underneath us – hopefully.

Ah! The sense of achievement when we made it to Gran's. What a tale of danger and intrepid exploration I would have to tell at school the next day! I wondered if Margaret would believe I'd seen a bear.

Gran was remarkably unperturbed though mildly surprised to see us. In the fifty years of living in that hill top farmhouse she'd seen it all. A little dot of woman, always dressed in something black and slightly shiny, like a half filled waisted bin bag, she didn't seem big enough to have given birth to eleven children, nine of them still surviving. She'd seen two world wars come and go with the Depression in between, and was slightly contemptuous of the burgeoning welfare state. Her nearest shop was two miles away in the valley, and there had always been little money to spare, so self-sufficiency was a way of life. Around the house chickens and ducks pecked, scratched and waddled, and pigs occupied the old stables. A large garden was a model of production, supplemented by the surrounding fields and hedgerows.

Grandad hardly ever appeared when we visited. He was a morose character, generally to be found in his workshop behind the house, tinkering with his brasswork hobby. When he came into the house at mealtimes, he sat in his own special chair at a separate table and rarely spoke. When he did speak, he scared me a bit. I could only stare at this enormous set of false teeth which, judging by the way they clacked together and hampered his speech, were much too big for his mouth to control. With his bald shiny head and wrinkled up eyes, he always made me think of Humpty Dumpty and how he must have looked after suffering his great fall.

The farmhouse was in the lea of the higher slopes, and that day the hillside around was almost bare of snow. However, Gran insisted on 'stocking us up well' for the return trip – hot tea always at the ready on the hob, and thick slices of homemade bread with pork dripping and dollops of rich brown meat jelly.

It became dark very soon after we arrived, so we literally had to retrace our footsteps to follow the way home, but Mam was well content. She knew that Gran was alright and we could look forward to a proper Christmas dinner. As she did every year, Gran had fattened the hens and made sure that there would be enough to go round the family at Christmas time, and though we had been challenged by the sudden snowfalls, here we were, two days before Christmas, with a lovely, plump, plucked and dressed hen under Dad's arm.

I think we must have been the first family in the country to take home a frozen chicken for Christmas dinner.

Fears and Fancies

Dad spent the war years in the Auxiliary Fire Service. I have no idea why he was not called up – possibly age (since he was over thirty when I was born), or possibly something medical. I do not know.

It was bedtime and I was very sleepy, but Mam was all of a twitter watching Dad put on his big rubber boots and the heavy dark coat of the Fire Service. It was just another ordinary bedtime, but I could not understand the fear and apprehension I sensed in Mam when it was Dad's duty night at the Fire Station.

The routine was normal, Dad would go off to spend his duty nights at the Fire Station, then later the sirens would sound, half waking me, signalling that Hitler was dropping bombs, aiming for the docks at Newport and Cardiff, the power station at Rogerstone or the steel works at Ebbw Vale. I reckoned they were all comfortably distant from our house, for it took nearly half an hour on the bus to get to Ebbw Vale, and the docks were further away. Fortunately, Hitler wouldn't know about the munitions factory at Pontypool, which was quite close, because it was secret. Margaret's Mam worked there and said so.

Anyway, after Hitler had dropped his bombs, which would miss of course, my Dad would go off in the fire engine and put out the fires. My Dad could do anything. If I ever woke in the night to the wail of the siren, and gave a thought to the town's coal mine being a target, I just rolled over and went to sleep again, knowing that Dad would deal with it. In any case, if there was any serious danger we would have had an air raid shelter somewhere, but we never even hid under the stairs when the siren went. A consensus among the neighbours had agreed that there was nothing in our street for Hitler to bomb, so why get nervous.

The whole business of war was exciting in a shivery kind of way. There was hiding in the long grass when any plane appeared in the sky, arguing over whether it was 'one of ours' or not and likely to fire on us. Then there was playing tag in the dark school air raid shelter, and suffering gas mask checks which were more unpleasant than scary.

Of course there was real tragedy too. Hardly more than a week went by it seemed without some child at school losing a father or close relative, but harsh and cruel as it was, there was less sense of shock and grief then. These adults had been out of the children's lives for very long periods of time, making brief appearances as strangers in uniform, so the shock of death didn't hit as hard or feel so final at the time. Meanwhile, the routine task of survival had to go on.

Real fear came from much smaller things. For Mam it was water. She could get quite panicky crossing a bridge over the river, and in summertime, to see me ankle deep in the stream was enough to get her going on about drowning and being swept away. Then again, even in the early post-war years, she was slow to accept that not every stranger was an enemy spy or Fifth Columnist.

She was most apprehensive about two strangers, regulars on our patch: the Sheikh selling things from a suitcase, and the Shoni Onion man. Well, one wore a turban (and you didn't see many of those going off to the pit every morning), and the other spoke barely any English, being French it was said. You couldn't get much more foreign and stranger than that, so Mam always whisked me indoors and out of sight when either appeared. 'You never know,' she hinted darkly. True, I never did, but it certainly never bothered me over much.

Early on in the war years, when Dad took on an allotment in the rough ground beyond the end of our garden, the land had to be cleared. In common with all the other allotment holders, Dad made a tump with the turfs of rough grass that he dug from the surface. These turfs were piled to form a hollow square with one side left lower than the other three so that the centre could be filled to make compost.

Before the composting got under way, we kids, being sort of honorary allotment holders by association, played 'being in the trenches and firing at the enemy,' and when the centres filled up, we stood on top of the turf embankment pushing each other off and shouting, 'I'm the king of the castle, get down you dirty rascal,' ready to repel all attempts to scale the tump.

Then the tumps got higher and the bigger boys in the neighbourhood came in to play serious war. There was only one thing for it. 'Can I play?' I said.

Paul, from next door, was a year older and much taller than I. He was thin enough to look almost waif like, but was tough as steel. He wore his dad's old cut down jacket with a swagger and his knowing sharp eyes stared almost through me as he calculated all the angles. In a nutshell, they were very short of enemy, but then again I was a girl. 'Tell you what,' he considered judiciously, 'if you can jump from the top of the tump, you can be Jerry.'

Easy, I thought, climbing on to my Dad's tump.

'Nah, thass easy,' said Paul. 'You gorra do my dad's tump.'

Now his dad's tump was higher than my head, and there was no way I could jump from the top of that. Paul shrugged and sloped off to continue lobbing grenades, masquerading as tufts of grass, at the advancing enemy hordes who were cunningly disguised as Tommy Crisp from No. 20 and Cliffie Sharp from next door but one. So I had no choice.

It took several attempts to reach the top of the tump. Even then, standing up was a wobbly effort, and the ground was incredibly distant. Someone had noticed me.

'Go on then. Jump! One, two three…'

Nothing. 'I wasn't ready. I can jump it easy.'

No going back now. This was real fear. The ground was hard, lumpy and a very long way off. I could break a leg and never, never, ever walk anymore, or I could die, and they'd put me in a nasty black coffin with the lid nailed on and I'd miss my birthday party.

It was the mocking counting that drove me on. It was fear, like a heavy gathering cloud ready to wrap and smother me in panic that shoved me in the back. I launched myself. The tufty grass was kind, but the ground still banged the breath from my body. I would not, must not, cry!

Then the fear fled as exhilaration swept over me. Now I was fully qualified to join the fighting troops. Right, come on, I thought, let's get this war fought and done with before teatime. I might be the enemy and so destined to lose, but I'd give them a run for their money.

In spite of the extra work of cultivating the allotment, Dad didn't neglect the front garden. This was part of the face we presented to the world, and in particular the neighbours. Every house had a privet hedge around its own square of lawn, and woe betide anyone who let either become unkempt. Like a dull brass letter box, an unscrubbed doorstep or 'a poor grain on the washing', it was the mark of a slattern in charge of the household.

Dad kept our hedge fairly low, just as high as the railings on the pavement side, with a higher decorative bush either side of the gate. This theme carried on around our circle of houses, with a few variations in height.

The highest hedge belonged to the Bowens. Mr and Mrs Bowen were of an older generation than our other neighbours, their only daughter married and moved away. They kept themselves very much to themselves and Mr Bowen was noted for his surly temper. Even when meeting in the street, a 'good morning' was extracted from him rather than being freely given. Any stray ball that bounced into the Bowen's garden stayed there on the remote off chance that Mrs Bowen might toss it back into the street sometime. Not one of us had the courage to knock on their door. They carried on an almost secret existence behind a high hedge and a tightly latched gate.

'Do you believe in ghosts?' asked Margaret, as we whiled away a sunny afternoon making daisy chains. I thought about it for a few minutes. I'd never seriously considered ghosts before, though there was that story about uncle Bill and uncle Lewis that was often trotted out at family gatherings, raising titters all round.

The two uncles, Bill and Lewis, then a couple of young blades, were walking home from Bargoed after a night out. First, there was the long open road from the valley towards their home 'up top'. Where the road levelled out, not far from home, there was just the old church and graveyard opposite the pub and a huddle of stone cottages. A small copse of trees was the only protection against an almost constant wind that swept down, unopposed, from the Brecon Beacons, whispering and moaning through the branches.

All the uncles had to do was to walk past the church and turn right, following the churchyard wall to the end, when the lights of home would be in sight, just five more minutes away.

They passed the side of the church where the trees were at their thickest and the cloudy moonlight at its gloomiest. The end of the wall was close.

Later, each would swear that a ghostly grey figure appeared on top of the wall. Bill ran for home with the devil at his heels, Lewis hared back to the pub.

'Ych, a sheep it was,' Granddad said disgustedly, and spat in the fire. 'Back you go boy, and fetch your brother home.'

The two brothers were a long time shouting to each other, well back from each end of the churchyard wall, and a much longer time coming home via a detour through boggy fields. The family were still making jokes at their expense about sheep that jumped up and said 'Boo' instead of 'Baa.'

I thought about the story as I studied my daisy chain. No one had ever proved it was a sheep on the churchyard wall, but then no one had ever proved it wasn't either. I came back to the present and Mar's question.

'Yeah,' I said, 'I s'pose so.'

Margaret savoured the moment.

'Well – don't tell anybody...'

(This was always a promising start.)

'There's a ghost in the Bowen's hedge,' she whispered triumphantly. A dramatic pause for the climax. 'I seen it.'

That clinched it. I looked across at the hedge; even in the afternoon sun, it was darkly dense, high and forbidding. Its shadow fell across what little could be seen of the front door and heavily net curtained windows like a sulky frown.

'Wass it like then?'

Margaret was not only vague in her description of the ghost, but also (for her) strangely reluctant. But I didn't need her description. In the fear that travelled up from the pit of my being and pricked tears at the back of my eyes, I knew instantly just what the ghost looked like.

The week before, Mam and Dad had taken me to the pictures. The film was not of any particular note, and in fact I was soon bored with watching the action and trying to follow the story. Then suddenly it caught my full attention as the scene shifted to a fairground, a place I had yet to experience since they had all disappeared 'for the duration'.

It was nighttime and a child was lost, the film expressing his sense of bewilderment quickening into fear. The fairground noises were no longer gaily strident, but threatening, harsh and overwhelming. Soon, the child was running in panic to leave his fear behind, till he had to stop for breath. Next to him was a glass case containing a large doll like a ventriloquist's dummy, laughing in a high pitched cackle and moving its head jerkily from side to side. Then, in the instant that the child paused, the dummy suddenly bent double, its face in close-up with the painted eyes rolling madly, and its laugh, now raucous and inhuman, deafening. The child screamed and I put my scarf over my eyes.

That night, as I lay in bed, I could still see that mad doll face so vividly. That 'thing' could be hiding, perhaps the other side of the tallboy, grinning to itself and waiting for the light to be switched off, before jerking its head close to mine with those insane eyes rolling. For a long time afterwards, without telling anyone why, I cried to have the light left on, and pulled the covers tight over my head every night.

The trouble was, with its inhuman powers, 'the thing' knew also where I went to school and where I played. Worst of all, it knew that the two high bushes of hedge on either side of our front gate were perfect hiding places for leaping out at me. I could avoid going into the air raid shelter at school (perfect for ambush), and all the other dark nooks and crannies, but the only way to reach the relative safety of my home was through the front gate. My only defence was to kick the gate open, then watch and listen for as long as it took to screw up courage for the sudden dash to safety.

Not a day went by without me being told off for not closing the gate behind me, but I never told anyone why I was so apparently thoughtless.

Now Margaret must have seen 'the thing', but I didn't ask for more detail. It would make my fears even more real. I didn't need a close description anyway of the ghost in the Bowens' hedge. I knew exactly what it looked like. Since a ghost or a 'thing' was not constrained by human limitations, it was a simple matter for it to be in two places at once. In fact, I realised with a sick lump in my throat, it probably lurked behind every hedge in our circle of houses. I was to carry that dread with me until I was tall enough to see over the tops of the hedges, all that is except the Bowens.'

Then, of course, there was the cricket ball. All through the summer the boys in the Circle set up their stumps on the green, always finding enough broken bean sticks to set out a wicket. Johny Meyrick also possessed a proper cricket bat and ball. But it was hard to make two teams from three boys. It meant that the fielder was a whole team on his own, and as the batsman got his eye in, tempers got shorter. The boys were forced to concede to the inevitable; they would have to admit girls.

There was fierce bargaining and hard negotiation. Kaff, lacking any great enthusiasm from the start, soon tired of this and went off to play three balls against the corner wall. Margaret and I were determined to join in the game, but on equal terms; we were not going to be given the run around (i.e. all the fielding and no batting), as the boys clearly intended, and of course we held the whip hand – no batting, no fielding.

The boys still wriggled, even after we had reached agreement. I was on Johny Meyrick's team, bringing the side up to three, except that, when the one batsman was in, everyone had to help with the fielding. Johny, as captain, batted first followed by Paul. When I saw his wicket go, I rushed for the bat, but before I could get my hands around it, Johny announced magnanimously that the score, six for two, was sufficiently solid for him to declare. This would give the other team, Cliffie and Tommy, plus Mar, a fair whack before we all rushed home to listen to the daily episode of 'Dick Barton – Special Agent' on the radio. This was mandatory listening for the pictures conjured up via the air waves made James Bond look like a wimp in a knitting circle (not that we'd ever heard of James Bond, or television for that matter).

I was furious, and refused to let go of the bat. Johny said, in a very superior way, that if you played cricket properly, you never argued with the umpire. I was obliged to point out that we didn't have an umpire, and from his partisan stance he hardly qualified for the position – or words to that effect. I think I stuck my tongue out for greater emphasis.

At this point, Margaret said that if we didn't get on with it no-one would get to bat before dark.

I patted the crease with a bat that I could barely lift, let alone swing, and Cliffie measured out his run up for bowling. With a shock, I realised that he was going to bowl overarm, and did I sense a hint of extra masculine aggression in his attitude? A grin split across his face as he built up steam, then he was coming at me like an express train. Blow the wicket. This was personal, and that ball was as hard as a brick with a rock in the centre. I cowered and gave a wild and desperate heave of the bat. The ball almost parted my hair, permanently, from my head. Cliffie bellowed 'Elbeedublew!!' and said I was out. What a relief! This was a pastime for masochists and idiots!

The Waterchute at Barry Island was a piece of cake after that. I'd heard rumours about the fairground re-opening after the war, and the barbed wire being removed from the beach, and ached to experience the seaside as only a nine year old can after a lifetime's denial.

We'd been up at the crack of dawn for our day trip to the sea. Today it would be barely an hour's drive by car, but then it was a proper journey involving careful planning.

First, we caught the early bus to Cardiff, a ride that was winding through and crossing the valleys, stopping more frequently than a chatty postman. Once there, we had to walk across town to join the queue for the Barry Island bus. This was why we'd been up at the crack of dawn. The Barry Island queue was always long (unless it was a rainy day), and, if the bus was full before our turn to get on, there was an hour's wait for the next one and a lot of calculating as to whether we'd get there before it was time to start the journey home.

We made it! This was clearly my lucky day. Not only had we caught the bus, but when we got to Barry Island I'd hardly had to whine and plead at all to get Mam and Dad to take me to the funfair.

This was nothing like the one in the film which had frightened me so much. The sun was shining, people were laughing and squealing with happiness and there was something new to discover round every turn – prizes to win, adventure, rides beyond imagination and the great mystery of candyfloss.

Mam and Dad thought they'd get away with a few sedate turns of the merry-go-round, but I had other ideas.

Dominating all the swings, stalls and roundabouts was a huge structure that surely touched the clouds. This was the stuff of speed beyond anything I'd known, of wildness and daring pushed to the limit. This was the Waterchute.

Mam took a lot of persuading. She was totally adamant about not putting such distance between herself and terra firma, and only let Dad take me after reeling out more instructions than an Army manual.

'Hold on tight. Hold Dad's hand. Don't look down. Just say if you want to get off. Sit tight. Keep your skirt tidy and don't scuff your shoes.' It was still going on as we boarded for the adventure trip of a lifetime.

Oh it was scary alright, but thrilling scary. This was flying like a bird with the speed of an arrow, or like a Spitfire even. All around was just sky, where we were level with the sun, where the stars would be at night. The rush of air, where there was none below, whipped my face, daring me to open my eyes; then came the moment of fear at its climax where we slowed and paused for a second, hung in space, before plunging towards the water. This was the very essence of the meaning of speed; to cease to be anything but part of that out-of-body rush of movement and clatter that could take us across the world in less than a minute if we failed to hit that still and glittering pool below.

The screams and screeches of joy all around snapped the tension like twanged elastic and carried us all laughing through the exit to where Mam stood white faced, her hair all wispy around her hat. 'Got no fear of nothing you,' she muttered accusingly. 'Why can't you play bucket and spade like the other kids?'

Didn't she notice anything? Didn't she notice that I wasn't a kid anymore, that I was a big girl now? She was almost right about fear though. For some time I had thought that I had conquered fear as a fully experienced entity. I had approached it, entered into it, through it and out the other side unscathed. Fear was licked by exhilaration inside me which was growing as I grew. Hitler was defeated, dead. There was no need to drop into the long grass anymore when a plane crossed the sky, no air raid shelter drill at school, no fear of bombing or shooting. The cricket ball seemed softer and lighter; dad's tumps were lower and easier to jump, 'the thing' shrank in size and lost its powers.

After another two summers of growing confidence, Mar, Joan and I talked about a really long bike ride. Joan was the one who inspired us. Although we were friends at school, Joan lived in a street beyond the Circle, and had often broken street gang rules to come and play with us in the Circle. Joan looked like a naïve, freshly baked little dumpling with a mass of curly black hair, but she was very practical and independent. Her mother had died while she was still an infant, but with the help of a nearby aunt, Joan and her father, a miner, managed pretty well.

Having left our village Junior School, we were ready to spread our wings and see what the world had to offer before the serious business of life at the Grammar School really bit. Joan reminded us that we now had full size bicycles at our command, and the world was our oyster. Distance had very little meaning, and anywhere outside our small valley was a foreign field.

Now that we were all three about to begin life at the Grammar School, we'd actually ridden to the school a couple of times for various Saturday morning sport activities. School was over four miles away, and having casually bragged about how easy it was, 'not even puffing' when we got there, the suggestion of going to Usk was attractive.

Why Usk? I'm not really sure except that it was the nearest place we could think of that had a river running free of coal sludge. This in itself made Usk sound glamorous.

We'd heard tales of the salmon that could be caught in the river Usk, and somehow that conjured a picture book pastoral scene in our minds, where the sun always shone, roses sprawled over every hedge and wall, and rabbits bobbed their tails across lush meadows.

I told Mam we were going to Joan's aunty's place at Newbridge. It wasn't really a lie. I just didn't tell her that we intended to keep going past Joan's aunty's for another six miles.

Mam wasn't sure at first. Newbridge was 9d on the bus, and that was a long way ticket. Still, it would keep me out of mischief and use up my energy.

We passed on the jam sandwiches on offer from each of our houses, and settled for meat paste ones with a bottle of Tizer. We were growing up now and our tastes were more sophisticated.

We set off with such eagerness! At first the ups and downs of the hills and the valleys by turn challenged and exhilarated. This was travel.

Soon we were in territory new to us, and this really felt like a long way from home. My legs pushed the pedals in a weary aching rhythm, with other parts of me joining in the protest. If only Joan or Mar had suggested turning back! But neither did, and I wasn't going to show cissy.

At last we coasted towards the outskirts of Usk. Here the road cut deep through steeped hedges rising from banks of wild daisies. The entrances to old cottages burrowed through the banks to flaunt their banners of roses and honeysuckle to all who passed by. As the slopes fell away here and there, we glimpsed flashes of the river as it bustled into town. It was becoming exactly like my picture book scene, and even the sun was shining.

When we came to cross the stone bridge leading to the little town square, we stopped as one, entranced. The rivers we knew in our own familiar valleys, or that we saw as we travelled to school, were all the same. They were channelled through the pitheads for washing the coal, and oozed rather than flowed, leaving slow silent swirls of thick black sludge along the banks. There were no fish. These were not places where you looked for any kind of life. Even the banks, frayed with dirty rocks and peppered with coal dust, were bare of grasses and plants. The nearest life of nettles and tough grasses was thin, starved and straggly, and there was no abundance.

Usk could not have been more different. Here the swift shallow water, more like splintered diamonds in the sun, dashed the pebbles and rocks to a bleached cleanliness as the current broke against them. Rushes and flowers of shapes and varieties strange to us dipped lazily along low green banks, sometimes cooling their blossoms in the quiet shallows.

Without a word spoken, we crossed the bridge and turned onto a footpath following the river's edge, content to walk now beside our bicycles. We savoured every sight and sound and movement to a background of pure water music, and didn't notice the man until he spoke.

'Having a nice ride girls?'

We turned in surprise. The man was casually dressed in open necked white shirt and trousers. Quite ordinary looking, a bit like Dad in fact.

I used Mam's criteria for judging people on first sight. His shoes were well polished, his shirt was clean, hair combed and he looked altogether 'tidy'. On the other hand, Mam was always reciting over and over again – 'don't talk to strangers'. Ah yes, but there were three of us, so it wasn't the same as being alone.

He laughed and joked a lot, telling us all about the town and the river, but insisted that we mustn't leave without visiting the castle. He told us how to get there, and strolled along with us, away from the town, till he indicated the start of a footpath that led away from the river up through thick woodland with no end in sight. He even pointed out a good place to leave our bikes, tucked away out of sight.

Here we parted company, and Joan, Mar and myself began the steep twisting climb.

'Dun like 'im,' said Mar flatly. Joan giggled. 'Reckon there is a castle at the top of this path then?'

'Well I never 'eard of it,' retorted Mar.

None of us had, but then we'd been growing up at a time when travel was limited by cost, fuel, the blackout and Hitler's bombers. Even the roadside signposts had been removed to confuse us.

I didn't know what to think; be open-minded or suspicious and condemnatory? How were you supposed to know? It was academic now anyway, since we were well up into the woods. It was cool and quiet here, with a lushness of leaf and blossom, stout tree trunks turning the path this way and that.

The castle appeared very suddenly, as the path twisted around a large oak then ended as if chopped. In this soft woodland setting the building really was quite enchanting. Much of it was a ruin, but the rambling outer walls were still quite sturdy and intact. Most of the interior seemed to consist of fine green lawns with grassy mounds where walls once stood and everywhere there were lavender bushes. Just one small section had defied the crumbling of age and siege, and this was actually lived in by two old ladies, who came twittering like starlings across the lawn to meet us. Dressed in grey floaty dresses with lots of lace, they blended perfectly with their surroundings.

One of them explained very firmly that the building was closed for the duration, but we were welcome to explore the grounds and they wouldn't charge an entry fee.

Clearly, they hadn't had many visitors recently. They were so excited, they fluttered around us, now more like cooing doves than starlings. When the novelty was exhausted they left us to roam the grassy-banked ancient walls on our own.

Meanwhile, the two ladies had settled themselves on either side of a large trug filled with lavender blossom. We were intrigued to watch them tying up bunches and then weaving them into be-ribboned lavender sticks. The purpose of this became plain when we made to leave. The doves turned hawkish in their sales pitch, and we suffered the embarrassment of explaining that we had no money. At least it cut out any lingering niceties in our departure.

The man was leaning against the oak tree where the path began. His greeting was again friendly and he was full of chatter, but now we all shared a sense of unease, heightened by the fact that there seemed to be nothing to feel uneasy about.

'That's a nice blouse you're wearing. Did you make it yourself?' He was smiling at me and I nodded. Then he fingered the button I'd left open at the neck, and ran his fingers along the material at the back, inside my blouse, touching my skin.

Suddenly I was frightened, my throat so tight I couldn't speak. My fear was gathering momentum because I didn't know why I was frightened. It was catching. Joan and Mar stood still and silent caught and held in my own fear. Mar broke the spell.

'C'mon,' she said, her voice loud and harsh. 'I'm off. You comin'?'

It was the jolt we needed, and it seemed to take the man by surprise. Mar led the way back down the path at a remarkable turn of speed, Joan and I running to keep up.

The man tried to keep pace with us, but was quickly left well behind stumbling on tree roots. When we hit the open river path, we stood panting, grateful for the nearness of some cottages no more than a shout away, and the sight of a car moving sedately along the road across the river.

When the man emerged from the woods, he simply turned along the path and walked rapidly out of sight, never looking at us once.

Somehow, the day had lost its thrill. Pleasure was gone. We were subdued as we collected our bikes, and in accord turned for home. We never even stopped to visit the town.

I felt both fear and guilt as we pedalled away. We all knew that we had learned a dangerous lesson, without fully understanding its nature, but soon I was becoming angry too.

There was comfort in my anger because I understood it. I thought of our excited planning and the enjoyment of our ride to Usk and all the things we had seen there. Then that man had robbed me of all the pleasures of the day. Now I could make a judgement of the day's events and had a right to be angry. And guilty too. But why? Guilty with the unease of bewilderment about something beyond my understanding.

To control these feelings, I had to keep them tight inside me and hang on to the justness of my anger. I think the others felt the same, for I knew instinctively that we would never talk about it, to each other or anyone else.

We pushed our bikes in silence up the first hill. Joan was the one who drew a line under the day's experience.

'I didn't like him neither,' she said firmly. Yes, there was no doubt about it, I had met fear in various forms and degrees and had to subdue or overcome it somehow, but on that day I discovered how effective anger can be as an antidote.

If ever I saw the ghost that lurked in the hedges and it tried to spoil my day, all I had to do was to get really angry and chase it away. Anger could be focussed and punched around inside my head until it was beaten.

Fairies in the Ether

There was absolutely no question that fairies existed. Apart from various pieces of circumstantial evidence – the sixpence that appeared under my pillow when I lost a tooth, the toys from Father Christmas that came every year during wartime when there were no toys in the shops – I knew that there were fairies. Margaret, who lived six doors away, had seen them in her garden, so it was unquestionably true.

Margaret was six months older than me, and had much more experience of life. She had seen a shooting star and had a piece of it to show me, and she had gone diving behind the barbed wire at Barry Island beach and was able to show me the huge piece of coral she had brought back. At least, she said it was coral, which saved me from making a fool of myself by mistaking it for a rough pebble from the stream.

So how could I doubt it when she told me about the three fairies living between the lilac bush and the privet hedge in her back garden? Her garden was good fairy country too. After the housework, cooking and her job at the munitions factory, Mar's mother had little time to spare for gardening, so apart from a couple of rows of potatoes and a patch of blackcurrant bushes, Mar's garden was left to run wild. I was very envious. Search as I might, I never saw any fairies in our garden. Mind you, they probably couldn't have stood all the digging, with Dad planting raspberries and potatoes and vegetables of every season.

'Come and get washed, we're going to aunty Lil's,' called Mam.

Oh cheese! Aunty Lil was one of Mam's younger sisters, and although we could see the mining village where she lived, straight across the valley, the downs and then the ups increased the distance considerably. It entailed a long walk in clean clothes and good shoes which mustn't be creased, scraped, scuffed, crumpled or marked in any way.

Off we went, across the field, and down the hill between high banks topped with disciplined hawthorns where there was always a slim chance of finding wild strawberries. Not today though. Then across the main road that led to town, to the footpath that twisted steeply down to the river. The path had once been cut through, leaving a very high bank on one side, way above my head with a row of sturdy beech trees leaning over to make a cool green tunnel.

Suddenly I was stopped dead in my tracks at the sight before me. Part of the bank had fallen away exposing a network of twisted roots, holed and laced with what Mam said was an old rabbit warren. But I knew she was completely wrong. This just had to be a place where fairies lived. It was exactly like a picture in one of my books, even to the detail of buttercups and bluebells growing in the field behind. A veritable fairy hat shop! The day was mine.

Even the fairy magic was working, because I skipped over the river bridge thinking of cracked crystal streams, not once leaning over to watch the thick black turgid sludge that came from the pit up the valley to slide under the span so lifelessly that it always made me shiver. That was reality; today I viewed the world through fairy tinted spectacles.

Now that we were at the bottom of the valley, we faced the prospect of taking the Hundred Steps leading towards the first of the houses on the other side of the valley.

In local geography, these were always referred to as the Hundred Steps, though I could never vouch for it because I always lost count when I tried checking. Certainly there were enough of them, going steeply up the hillside through a grove of trees, thick with silver birch and ferns, to warrant flopping on the grass at the top until knees stopped shaking and we could speak without gasping. Odd, now, to think that was the way to and from work for many of the pit men.

The rest of the afternoon was just a fret of impatience, waiting for Mam to finish drinking tea and gossiping with aunty Lil. I couldn't wait to get back home so I could boast to Mar about my colony of fairies – I wouldn't tell her exactly where they were though. Quite a triumph of a day really.

It was not long after this that I figured I didn't have to go so far afield to find the fairies. I was listening to the radio. Not such a casual business as it is today. First the radio, or rather the wireless, had to be switched on in time to warm up. It whined and whistled and crackled in protest at being disturbed as the knobs were finely tuned to accommodate intelligible sound, then a quick sharp tap on the side and we had it. But it did mean sitting almost ear to the set for the reception to have any clear meaning. I listened to uncle Mac and Tales of Romany, lost in other worlds, and then for the first time became irresistibly curious about the how and the why of radio. And why was it called wireless when an electric lead plugged into the wall socket ran into the back of the set, plain as day? With my fingers, I traced the electric wiring from the plug behind the curtains and peered behind the set. To my great excitement, this one look confirmed a suspicion I had had for some time.

There was the smallest of gaps where the back of the wireless was fastened to the set, and without doubt, a chink of bright light could be seen inside, with shadows and shapes to guess at. There was flickering movement too, all indicating signs of life. Someone was definitely living in there! They had to be very small of course, but they were there alright.

I had puzzled since the first time of listening about the voices that came from the set. After all, how could they just come from the air when I often couldn't hear Mam from the end of the garden?

My suspicions had been aroused by odd remarks emanating from the wireless from time to time, like 'don't do that' when I thought no-one could see what I was up to, or a cry of 'bed time children' just as Mam entered the room with my nightie in her hand. Now I knew. There were tiny, tiny people living in there, all mod cons and fully furnished, only needing us to switch on the set and provide the electric light for them to see by and start performing. This was a really thrilling discovery. They must be even smaller than the fairies! Oh what a magic world indeed we lived in if, like Mar and I, people only used their eyes to look for the magic.

I don't know what sort of people live in the back of TV sets, but certainly, with all of modern technology at their command, they are unable to provide anything like the vivid and utterly believable pictures of the wireless.

A Thirst for Adventure

'Pop' was a very evocative word. Mar and I sat on the warm kerbstones which marked the border of the grassy circle that was our world of play. At various times we had swum through the grass facing the dangers of the oceanic deep (and hidden turds of horse manure), we had batted for England in it, won Wimbledon, picnicked on desert islands, fought back Nazi hordes, created snow supermen and gathered arms full of dog daisies.

Now the weather was hot, and nursing our dolls back from the brink of death had been thirsty work. Mam had given us a bottle of 'council pop' from the kitchen tap, but it had soon become lukewarm in our sticky hands and no stretch of the imagination could turn it into ginger beer or anything in the least exotic.

We had a whole day to wait before the pop man made his weekly delivery, to which the wooden crate full of empty bottles, just inside the front door, bore witness. It also marked part of the first expansion in daily life after the worst constrictures of the war.

'I like dandelion and burdock best.' Of this I was quite certain. 'Nah, Tizer,' said Mar. I thought about the golden sweetness of Tizer compared with the rich brown dandelion and burdock and its faintly liquorice flavour. At that moment I would have settled for either one.

'My aunty said the pop man got ice cream soda – and cherry!' Ice cream soda? This was beyond me. You couldn't get ice cream in a bottle, and even if you could, it would melt when you tried humping round the streets on the back of a lorry. Not that I knew much about ice cream.

Apparently it had been one of the first luxuries of life to be sacrificed to the war effort, and I had yet to taste it. However, there were times when I suspected that Mar was over-generous in the substance of knowledge that she passed on.

It was a hot bright afternoon but we were as flat as the dregs in the pop bottle. Our day's derring deeds had petered out. We had mastered and controlled within our grassy play circle everything on land and sea as we patrolled in the guise of two Spitfires, and had left the skies clear of any threat to man or beast.

'Less go down the oak tree,' Mar suddenly hissed. It was tempting. The huge old oak was at least half a field away beyond my limit of roaming, which gave an edge of excitement to the idea. This idea was not only blossoming, in our discussion of the pros and cons, it was growing a side shoot. A picnic no less!

Mam was quite amenable to making us a couple of jam sandwiches and finding a paper bag for a bit of glamourisation. We were almost out of the front gate before she realised that we weren't going to sit on the front lawn and nibble like little ladies.

'Going up Mar's house,' I yelled towards the kitchen door before we could be questioned too closely. That was quite acceptable, and true enough – well for starters anyway. We replenished our water bottle at her house, then skulked around the corner towards the field where the oak tree beckoned. This tree was the biggest in the world, bigger than any of the bushes in the gardens where we played, looming larger than Mrs. Bowen's privet hedge. It even dwarfed the fruit trees in Gran's garden.

The shape of the stout trunk lent itself naturally to playing house in quite a grand fashion, meting out jam and justice, washing and wisdom, tea and tidbits of gossip, creating world order in the manner of our elders. We drank Tizer, dandelion and burdock, lemonade and even the mysterious ice cream soda, all from the same bottle of 'council pop', and jam sandwiches yielded slices of roast beef that only existed in the imagination.

And then we found the rope. It was old and frayed and had probably lain in the grass all summer, but it was long enough to loop over the lowest branches of the tree. Mar, with her six months maturity over me, could do proper knots, and – hey presto! – our loop of old rope transformed into

Spitfires that could really fly, without our feet or any part of us touching the ground. Oh heady stuff! If we'd known anything of champagne we'd have drunk that too from our water bottle.

The rope broke quite suddenly, and I tumbled to the ground like a Spitfire with its wings gone. That certainly levelled off the excitement, but, what was more to the point, my foot had slid through a cow pat on landing, and now my white socks were well and truly plastered.

We both knew the score on white socks. Clean white socks folded neatly above the ankle were the indisputable mark of a nice girl and a lady in the making. Clean darned socks expressed virtue in the act of darning. Dirty socks, or (unthinkably) no socks at all showed up a sluttish and slatternly mother. So I was in real trouble – my socks were not just dirty, but stinking.

Mar, considering the problem and its repercussions, drank half of what was left of the water and gave me the other half. We turned towards home with an empty paper bag and I with the taste of flat warm water in my mouth. Then one of us, I can't remember which, had a brainwave. The solution to my troubles lay in the golf pond and all that clean running water!

We turned back, going even further than the oak tree and passed through the kissing gate at the edge of the golf course. A footpath sloped gently down into a little 'cwm' where a cluster of ash and beech trees shaded a small spring. This flowed into a lively little stream which sought its way across the golf course to the coal thickened river in the valley below. Not far from the spring, the 'cwm' levelled slightly and the stream paused in its meandering to form a pond, usually quite shallow but which could deepen dramatically after winter rains.

By this time, both my socks were well and truly cow patted, and without a second's hesitation I peeled them off and waded into the pond, scrubbing them vigourously in the water. Indeed they were almost clean, and the water was so cool; I wiggled my feet well down in the sand bottom.

The one thing we hadn't thought about was drying. Going home with wet socks would give the game away completely, and since the golf pond was even more out of bounds that the oak tree, the consequences did not bear contemplating.

We had no way of knowing the time, but it was late afternoon by now and the sun had lost its brightness; there were more long shadows than patches of light in the 'cwm', and although I had hung my socks on a bush, we were in for a long wait. Apprehensively, I wondered if Dad would be home from work yet. We started to worry about it getting dark. Neither of us fancied the walk across two fields in the blackness of night – an open invitation to any passing neighbourhood ghost, hinted Mar.

But rescue was at hand. Coming towards us, peering into bushes and round every tree, came Dad. Forgetting our plight, we both ran joyfully to meet him, I waving my socks in the air with great enthusiasm. He was very quiet though – not a word from him in fact, and we trotted back each of us holding one of his hands and chattering nervously to fill the silence.

Mar's mother met us at her gate. She nodded her thanks to Dad and marched Mar indoors. I began to get very worried.

Mam had also been waiting at the gate, but before we arrived, had gone into the kitchen to stoke the boiler of her anger, fear, worry and frustration. I got it full blast, and some of it stuck for years.

'… all the circle out looking. P'lice it would have been next, and we've never had a p'liceman at the door in all the time we've lived here. Drown in that old pond you could. Look at the state of you. What will people think, I don't know…'

She'd taken a good long breath before she started and was clearly well settled into her theme for a good long time. Dad was just staring at me as I stood there, rather indifferently, still trying to conjure up and re-live some of the fun of the afternoon.

Suddenly, he whisked me off my feet and across his knees. The spanking I got was short but brought a glowing blush to my backside. Then I was bundled to bed.

This was the one and only time in my life that Dad ever raised a hand to me and was therefore a lesson I never forgot; when you get stuck in a hole don't keep digging and especially don't wave the shovel about.

Making Do

'Sit up tidy and look quiet. And don't make a mess.'

Mam did not understand the artistic temperament. Her driving concern was to create an even rhythm of family life which did not untidy the house, crease the embroidered linen cushion covers or cause dirty marks and smudges to appear on anything that had just been scrubbed or polished.

Kitted up in a floral overall and matching mob cap, which restrained two rows of dark brown sausage curls disciplined in metal curlers, she was a formidable and implacable enemy to any form of dirt or mess that dared to test her skill or resources.

'Oh there's a mess! What are you doing?' Actually, I was looking at my attempt to create a Chinese lantern. It hadn't been easy, unlike the one I'd made at school, months ago, in the run up to Christmas. Then we'd each been given a measured piece of stiff, coloured paper, a pair of scissors and access to the classroom pot of glue, fold, cut, open, stick – and voila! A dainty creation of lightness and colour.

Now I only had newspaper to work with, and my flour and water sticking paste had turned out lumpy. Then I kept losing my embryo lantern in the newspaper covering Mam had put over the kitchen table. She must have used the paper output of an entire tree.

Gay colours, I thought, that would make everything come right. Red, blue, yellow – my enthusiastic onslaught on my paintbox produced a mass (or should it be mess?) of weak rainbow hues, at which the paper surrendered its limpness to complete sogginess. My lantern had given up the ghost without ever seeing the light of day.

'There's a proper mess you've made,' repeated Mam, brutally truthful.

'I'll fetch a cloth. Now you go and shell the peas I picked for dinner.'

Surveying the remains of my mushed up never-would-be lantern, she added, 'Sit on the doorstep and do it.'

I was quite glad to escape my failed effort, but shelling peas did little for the imagination.

The garden was Dad's weapon against Hitler. We were 'Digging for Victory', clearing the lawn and flower beds to produce enough fruit and vegetables to feed ourselves and to trade with the neighbours. We'd show the government how to win the war!

In the meantime, the peas needed my attention. The first pod was only just beginning to swell, full of young, juicy peas, vividly green with burgeoning vitality. I had to test the flavour. A tentative nibble, and the flavour burst free as my taste buds blossomed with delight. These peas passed the test of perfection without fault, as did the next crisp pod-full, and the next, until my pleasure was almost sated. Life was beginning to look rosy again.

'Plenty of pods you've done there!' Mam's voice brought me to earth. 'But where's the peas?' There followed a lecture on eating all peas and no dinner, and retribution in being sent off down the garden to replenish the sad little mound of peas in the basin. I was supposed to do this without getting my shoes mucky and bringing mud in the house. I'd be lucky to escape without a lecture on 'Do you know how many coupons a pair of shoes are?'

The trouble with clothing coupons was that, no matter what you wanted to buy, there were never enough of them, and as Mam so often remarked, the situation wasn't helped by me growing so fast. When rationing started, I wasn't even out of my pushchair, but once I really started running around I seemed to grow out of things in no time. And there were the normal daily hazards; kerbstones, footballs and hopscotch stones scuffed my shoes, hedges, bushes, railings and doorknobs pulled at my buttons with resulting damage. I'd heard more mutterings about false hems, gussets, darning and 'letting out' than a convention of East End tailors. New clothes were rare.

This was a time when aunty Gwen and aunty Doreen were in their element. Aunty Gwen was the perpetual knitter, stitcher and embroiderer, while aunty Doreen was the spark of ideas and initiative and was also the sewing machine operative.

They'd always had a penchant for saving things that might come in handy, and the outbreak of war with its shortages and scarcities left them thoroughly vindicated with a determination to advance the fight against waste. The kitchen drawers had paper bags and pieces of string of every length and size which gave me my first lessons in patience as I endeavoured to smooth out creases and unravel long tied knots.

The big Victorian dresser which took up one side of the living room housed Gran's best dinner service, the odd spaces between the various plates and dishes filled with jars of buttons. I loved being allowed to play with these buttons. They all had stories attached to them of weddings, funerals, army life and family gatherings, being the last remnants of clothes that had been worn with gaiety, solemnity, joy and duty. The bedrooms held cupboards and chests and tucked away suitcases, all with various treasures of outmoded dresses, beads, buckles, skeins of wool and embroidery silks rich with the scent of mothballs.

I loved the old curtains and snippets of dress material that re-appeared in their new incarnations as dolls, exuberant in a mixture of colours and designs that put grey wet afternoons to shame. It was the big things that made me apprehensive.

We arrived, as we always did, at Gran and Grandad's house 'down below' at teatime on Saturday afternoon. Mam followed aunty Gwen and Doreen into the kitchen, with much rustling of paper bags and hushed voices. This was a normal ritual, since no-one in our world, in the era of rationing, would dream of accepting hospitality without reciprocating with a gift of food or drink. Sometimes we could offer a couple of tomatoes from Dad's greenhouse, a bag of Welsh cakes, a precious egg cocooned in a twist of newspaper or, most generous of all, a tin of fruit.

Mam and the aunties trooped back into the living room and looked at me. They twirled me round slowly, like Mam did when she was looking for dirty marks on her treasured silver cake stand. Then I had to stand against the wall to be measured. I knew from long experience that they had come across some item of clothing which would 'do lovely' for me, with a little bit of altering.

My heart sank. Over a period of many months, the marks had crept up the wall indicating the intervals between measurings, but one thing was quite remarkable. No matter what aunty Gwen and Doreen had in mind for me, whether it was a coat, skirt, blouse or petticoat, they only ever measured height. Since aunty Gwen in particular was a very large lady, the results of the measuring and altering were often quite bizarre, so I was dreading the outcome of all these shenanigans.

A week passed, and off I went with Mam again for Saturday afternoon shopping, then back to Gran and Granddad's at teatime.

As we puffed up the last stretch of hill towards their house, Mam prepared the ground with great subtlety.

'If you get given anything, you remember to say thank you and look pleased.' Long pause. 'Even when you don't like it, say thank you.' Trouble ahead. I knew now that I was in for something I definitely wouldn't like.

Aunty Gwen and Doreen for the most part behaved as sensible spinsters should, but when we arrived they were animated to the point of giggliness, and tea was quite a chatter clatter affair. It was hard to follow the darting conversation around and across the table, with plates and cups to-ing and fro-ing for yet more wafer thin bread with its gossamer of butter, and repeat cups of tea. At last the pace slowed and the teapot was empty.

Time to go home. Just for a moment I thought I had escaped whatever fate and the aunties had been working on all week. I was taken to the sweetie tin on the mantelpiece where the week's sweet ration for the household had just replenished the contents, and was told I could pick two sweets to take home. This was 100% increase on what I was usually given! Clutching a toffee and a mint gob stopper I duly said 'thank you' with genuine enthusiasm and thought we'd be away.

Then aunty Gwen appeared with a large ginger bundle clutched to her chest.

'Good tweed this is,' she said, 'bought pre-war, not on coupons.'

Brisk hands thrust me inside the flamboyant hairy mass. Aunty Gwen enveloped me in her ample curves, breathing excited 'Oohs' and 'Aahs'.

The tweed coat, as my covering turned out to be, had needed some alteration. Apart from moving the buttons some considerable distance, the aunts had cut about ten inches off the bottom and almost as much off the sleeves.

I looked in horror at the old elbow creases in the sleeves, resting just above my wrists, and I could feel the intended waist line buttoning around my bottom. I had to appear in public in this thing!?

Mam and the aunts cooed and twittered with pleasure at the quality of the tweed and the warmth in it, while I was so panicked I almost forgot to say 'thank you'. Mam was so pleased she insisted I kept the 'thing' on to wear home, creeping through the dusk like an ancient wrinkled moggy.

As winter encroached, it was surprising that I never caught pneumonia, for whenever I was made to wear the coat, I took it off as soon as I had turned the first corner and carried it like a parcel of dubious content.

It was possibly this experience, and other similar ones involving shirts and moth balled dresses, which encouraged me to sew.

Aunty Gwen had shown endless patience in teaching me simple embroidery and how to crochet, and soon I was doing real sewing in junior school. With a scarcity of materials in wartime this was pretty limited, though I did produce a rather unexciting traycloth.

Wool was more accessible and could be unravelled and used over again, so we quickly graduated to knitting. Full marks to Miss Pritchard, my class teacher, who was an iron corseted blend of common sense and discipline. Knitting sessions with her were an experience of boredom tempered with faint curiosity as we produced row upon row of conformity. It was hardly a surprise to discover eventually that we had each produced a scarf.

At least the next item had a different colour of wool. We learnt a few more basic stitches too, but it was still a matter of patient repetition, row upon row, with hardly any variation except for 'do six rows of stocking stitch, and cast off one at each end' or 'do another ten rows'. It was like a life sentence on the chain stitch gang, especially since I had no idea of what I was supposed to be making. Nor did anyone else.

We all thought 'gloves' at first, our obvious guess after the scarf experience, but as a variety of shapes began to grow, clearly a wrong one. More curious still, there were no two shapes the same within the class knitting production, and as one piece was finished, we were given more wool and the whole process began again.

Towards the end of the autumn term I had amassed a bag full of assorted knitted pieces of no recognisable shapes, some blue, some white, and no hint of the whole they might form. Boredom won over excitement on the finishing straight. I was only informed it was the finishing straight after I'd completed it and had to hand over to Miss Pritchard my bag full of blue and white pieces. Miss Pritchard ran a tight ship; no talking, no slacking, no slouching and no answering back – as if anyone dared!

Now that my knitting was accepted as complete, I was free. I could enjoy the end of term and the build up to Christmas. I was a spectator of Miss Pritchard applying her implacable will to the more tardy and untidy knitters until every girl in the class had filled a bag of pieces to Miss Pritchard's satisfaction. As I got on with the task of making Christmas paper chains to hang around the classroom walls, I decided that I would never do any knitting ever again for the whole of my life, even when I became as ancient as Mam or any of my aunties.

The last morning of term started clear and frosty. Every stretch of pavement on the walk to school had a slide to whiz along, and the white crusted sloping playground was ready for polishing with our metal studded winter shoes.

In spite of the fun, I was glad to tumble into the classroom with its glowing one piece of coal fire and brass rimmed fireguard always pleasantly warm to the touch, while eddies of warmth and cold draughts combined to make our paper chains sway limply.

But in an instant my pre-occupation with cold and warmth vanished. The mantelpiece above the fireplace was crammed. Normally it was the same cold porridge colour as the walls, bare except for three of Miss Pritchard's books on one side and a box of chalk on the other. Today it was like Noah's Ark in technicolour. There were animals of very shape, variety and colour, all knitted and each with a name pinned to it.

We were hustled to our seats, for once stilled and speechless, then Miss Pritchard called us to her desk one by one. I think a week went by before my name was called, and I was handed a blue and white penguin, upright and firm yet soft and cuddly with his cotton wool stuffing. It had to be, yet I couldn't believe that my odd shaped pieces of knitting had been combined to make this gorgeous creature.

Miss Pritchard, as it turned out, had pieced together all these bits of animals and then added the finishing touches, like mine had with his lovely curving black felt beak, shining button eyes, and sturdy card stiffened webbed feet. Miss Pritchard was a miracle worker and I was a believer.

Mam was able to boast about my skill and talent for weeks, which didn't do me any harm at all. Every stitch and every row of knitting had been worth it.

Miss Pritchard, though quite unaware of it at the time, had done exactly the right thing to soothe an old but still aching hurt.

When I had been much younger, in my early school days, I had received among all the other homemade toys one Christmas my 'Dak Doll'. Since practically the only material in reasonable supply at the time was 'blackout' material for making windows lightproof at night, it was used by home dressmakers with great enterprise and initiative. Thus, when I woke on this particular Christmas day, and dived into the bulging pillowcase at the end of my bed, it was inevitable that a piece of 'blackout' in some inventive shape or form would emerge.

But my delight way outstripped my expectation. He had a huge round black face plastered with an edge to edge smile. White cloth buttons, stitched in the centre, formed his twinkling eyes, and his hair was like a crinkly wool coat collar, the same as the one aunty Gwen used to wear. And such style and colour in his clothes! In his blue satin trousers, red cummerbund and purple velvet jacket he put wartime drabness to shame. It was love at first hug tight.

I was young enough to have difficulty with words like 'black' so this flamboyant creation, was simply and instantly named 'Dak Dolly,' and Dak Dolly he remained through all our days together. He was a loyal companion who never left my side; he was cuddly and comforting and never cross. Never shocked by anything I told him, he never betrayed a secret or criticised. He was the perfect friend.

Our parting was swift and unexpected. We were both sitting on the back doorstep, enjoying the late morning sun together in harmonious silence, as friends do. Dak Dolly was a little shabby by this time. His hair and one eye had worked loose, and one arm seemed to have a perverse will of its own in flopping about at strange angles to his body. The best to be said about his clothes was that they reflected a certain distressed gentility, or what Mam called 'dropping to bits.' But we were just as happy together, and his beaming smile never drooped or faded.

Mam was making a good gravy for dinner. I could smell its promise of rich meaty flavour from where I sat. There might or might not have been any meat, but at least we had plenty of fresh vegetables from the garden with unlimited meaty flavoured gravy to mash them up in.

It was possibly the good beefy aroma that attracted the dog. He suddenly appeared around the corner of the house, shuffling and shaggy, his nose testing the air ahead of him. I'd never seen him before. I was intrigued.

He paused at the step and studied me with languid brown eyes, half hidden in tufts of fur. Then he noticed Dak Dolly, with his wide-eyed happy face and his one wild arm nonchalantly tucked through a loose loop of hair, as if raised in welcome.

It was all too much for the dog. He pounced, and the last I saw of Dak Dolly was a flash of purple jacket as the dog carried him off through the gap in next door's hedge.

Despite uproar and outcry and Dad's quiet diligent searching, there was never a trace of dog or Dak Dolly. I was bereft and inconsolable. I had other dolls, but never a friend and companion like Dak Dolly.

Then Penguin appeared in my life. He didn't smile, but his broad based beak and deep shiny eyes made him look so wise, far beyond my years, and no matter what I said to him, he was incapable of anger. By this time I was too old to carry my new friend about with me, so he spent his days in my bedroom, contentedly standing on his wide flat feet, just thinking.

I still couldn't believe that this beautiful amazing creature had evolved from all those odd pieces of blue and white knitting that had seemed so tedious a task at the time. I had to know the secret. From now on I would knit and sew until I could really understand the complicated things like

fence across the field, and this was followed by three large Nissen huts, sprouting overnight like giant misshapen toadstools.

For a while, we walked to town along the street passing the front of our house, avoiding the Showfield. The next time we came home through the field, I was outraged to discover a wooden fence alongside the public footpath, way past the big oak tree and the other kissing gate, right to the top of the field. Inside the fence, beside the three Nissen huts, were half a dozen small planes, tents everywhere and men in strange uniforms. We'd heard rumours of them, but never seen them until now – they were Americans.

On the whole, the excitement of the sudden arrival of the Americans was quite mild. The town had already absorbed several Italian families who opened their cafes as the industrialists opened the mines, then there were the Poles who came to work in the mine (the Bevan Boys as they were known), and a fair share of evacuees from as far away as Dover and Liverpool with accents just as strange as the American drawl.

The natural exuberance of the Americans seemed to generate extra gossip. This always stopped abruptly when 'little ears' were about, with the occasional word, more often muttered sideways through tight lips, left hanging in the air. These were words like 'nylons', 'jitter bugging' and 'three months gone'. They all sounded pretty dull to me though. For us kids there were only two words synonymous with Americans, and they were 'chewing gum'.

At every possible opportunity we pestered them. 'Got any gum, chum?' was the newest and most exciting game. If one of our Allies was cornered and had no gum about him with which to buy his freedom, he would lean down, point to some poor unsuspecting compatriot of his in the distance and whisper to the nearest kid, 'You see that guy? Well, his name is Wrigley and his pa makes all the gum in America.'

It never failed. As foreigners, and in uniform, they all looked alike to us anyway, so armed with this information, the lead kid was off, the rest of us in hot pursuit like wasps to a jam pot. The next Yank never stood a chance. As a whole, they only survived to take part in the war as the novelty of chewing gum began to wane.

I wished we could have the field back as it had been, not given over to the War Effort, like old iron railings and flower gardens and new clothes.

But there was one consolation as the fortunes of war ebbed and flowed. 'My' corner of the field was apparently of no use in bringing about Hitler's downfall. When the short precious season was right, I could still whip my feet through the grass and lie in perfect peace as the harebells nodded in gentle harmony about my face. The world might have changed, but one tiny bit of it was still the same – and still mine.

The summer flowers all too soon gave way to berries and fruits in the fields and hedgerows, and then it was winter with its bareness and deep darkness.

Indoors, we would manage in the afternoon gloom for as long as we could. This was only in part for economy's sake, because before we dared switch on any light, all the blackout curtains had to be tightly drawn across every window. I wasn't absolutely sure, but it was possible that one of Hitler's planes was lurking up in the darkening sky, just waiting for one little glimmer from our house to set his bomb sights on us. Mind you, I think Mam was more scared of the warden, Bevan the Blackout to us, making his rounds ready to yell, 'Put that light out!' Showing a light was presumably so terrible a crime that I never knew what happened to anyone who transgressed. Certainly I knew of no one who dared test the system.

There was no other escape from the dark. With no street lights, we moved cautiously after night fell, only hand torches guiding us, white paper taped across the glass to reduce the glow to little more than a less dark shadow. I very quickly knew every chipped paving slab, each bent piece of railing and each odd shaped bush on the way to friends' and relatives' houses.

As winter deepened and the weather worsened, even the wild mountain ponies got fed up. Before it was properly light, they were down among the town gardens, taking shelter from the walls and anything they could eat from the vegetation. Dad always shooed them off out of our garden every morning, but seemed to have some sympathy for their plight. And they always left generous, even priceless appreciation for their breakfast – manure.

Of course, everyone was doing their bit to 'Dig for Victory'. Flowers, shrubs and lawns disappeared to be replaced by anything that was edible. What we didn't eat immediately we pickled, bottled, jammed, salted or dried. By the time the poor ponies arrived they were lucky to find anything bar a few leeks and cabbage stalks.

So, Easter Sunday in church was an event of more than special celebration. Apart from what we were taught at Sunday school, the strictures of those wartime days added so much more to the event.

Following the family tradition set by Gran 'down below', we had a windowsill to decorate in the church. On Easter Saturday I went to Gran's house, going the long way round, across the edge of the wood, arriving with my arms full of yellow catkins and silver pussy willows. Gran and aunty Gwen had baskets all packed and covered ready to rattle and chink our way down the stone path to the church. Gran also had one huge quiet basket tightly packed with flowers.

It was a mark of social standing to take part in the decorating of the church. Vicar's wife and hierarchy did the altar and chancel. Church warden's wife did the font, and the rest of us did the best we could with the wide stone windowsills.

First, we unpacked the baskets. With all the flowers was a collection of empty paste pots and jam jars, the cause of our noisy progress to church. My first task was to go foraging through the boxes at the back of the vestry for more jars. There were never enough jars for all the flowers and greenery, so it was an 'elbows out, no holds barred' effort.

The problem was that everyone was collecting glass jars for one reason or another. As Brownies and Girl Guides, we each endeavoured to take at least one jar apiece to our weekly meetings for the 'War Effort'. I never questioned this. The 'War Effort' was both complete explanation and reassurance for any request that was made of us.

Jars were a bit of a puzzle though, as even my childish imagination could not visualize Spitfires, battleships, tanks, bombs or bullets made of re-fashioned jars. Maybe they filled them with Mrs Evans' horrible sugarless marrow jam and poisoned the enemy. However, it was enough that the request was made and we all responded.

Not all the jars were to be hurled at Hitler though. Aunty Gwen and Doreen had a small horde for each of these such occasions like when the church needed to be decorated.

Mam had a box of jars tucked away for 'jam and bottling'. They were valuable for preserving an excess of garden produce and this store would not even yield to the needs of the church. They were even more valuable when a neighbour was short of jars for preserving the garden produce. The neighbour would be forced to beg any spare jars, and since no one would dream of going to beg or borrow empty handed, Mam often gained a bonus of extra fruit or vegetables – or even a cup of precious sugar.

All this helped to make me feel very important and responsible when I went jar hunting behind the church vestry. Inevitably, the jar rivalry spread to the decoration.

'Mrs Williams' window is coming nice. Needs a bit more colour in the centre though.'

'Pity about the Misses Thomas' daffs.'

'Too showy that one. She'll be trying to outdo the altar her.'

The whispers hung in the air, unknowingly tuned to childish ears, and I determined that our window would be the best. I carried water and jars enough to fill a cathedral, or so it seemed, until at last my moment came, after Gran and aunty Gwen had made lush arrangements of tall spring flowers, boughs of greenery and my catkins and willows.

I lined up my paste pots and spread out my cherished bundles of primroses, violets, primulas, grasses and assorted green leaved twigs all provided for me by Gran. Thinking hard on the word 'artistic' that I'd heard aunty Gwen bandying about, I divided my flowers and filled the jars so that the front of the windowsill would be a mass of tiny blooms, cunningly concealing all the jam jars behind, glorious in their colour, swathing across the stonework as if bursting from it to flaunt their full beauty. At least, that's the way I saw it.

When aunty Gwen was satisfied, apart from our display and the heavy scent of narcissi, we left without a speck of evidence of our activity left behind. Newspaper went back for lighting the fire or to make spills for lighting the gas or Grandad's pipe; twigs and branches would become kindling, and who knew where string and brown paper would end up. The odd spare jar went behind the vestry, in a gesture of Christian unselfishness, and as an example to myself.

I always loved Easter Sunday. Sometimes it might be cold enough for scarves and gloves, or teeming with rain, but it was still a decisive end to winter.

Mam, like most mams then, always had a new hat, or more often than not, a renewed hat, designed and fashioned by adding to or taking from a long outdated model, and I always had a new one too, knitted by aunty Gwen. If it was cold or wet all the hats made a grand entrance into the church, bursting forth in their glory from under scarves and umbrellas as they passed through the porch.

For once, the usual morning service scents of mothballs and eau-de-cologne were subdued almost to the point of extinction by the rich cocktail of perfumes wafting from the massed spring flowers that filled every ledge with curve and colour to delight the eye.

Between being nudged to 'sit still, stop turning round, don't fidget, don't sniff, blow your nose', I managed to check every decorated window against our own. Impossible to pick the best, but ours was certainly up to comparison with any other.

But one thing I could never cease to wonder and puzzle at. Everywhere, people had dug up flowerbeds, bushes and shrubs and planted potatoes, cabbages, fruit bushes and onions. So where did all those hundreds of flowers come from?

Life on a Knife Edge

For some reason, which I never pondered, we didn't possess a carving knife. Apart from the usual table cutlery, we just had 'the big knife' and 'the little sharp knife', and these two implements catered for all the culinary activity in our house. 'The little sharp knife' peeled, chopped and sliced and even helped to extricate garden vegetables until it became so blunt we had to sharpen it on the concrete edge of the doorway or the stone step outside the kitchen. 'The big knife' was a bone handled bread knife, with a serrated edge blade, and since ready sliced bread was yet to come and revolutionise our lives, we depended upon 'the big knife' to hack our bread into crusty, doorstep slices. With the butter ration being so very scant, the bread was purposely cut thick anyway, and we learned to relish toppings like 'thunder and lightning' – condensed milk dribbled over the bread and sprinkled with cocoa. Golden syrup was pretty good too, but best of all was the Sunday night gob stopper supper of an even thicker than usual slice of bread spread with soft pork dripping, dotted with pieces of the stiffly gelled pork juices all well salted.

The only food that resisted attack from either of these knives was cheese. This arrived every week in our delivered grocery order. The only choice was cheddar, on ration of course, and it was chipped from a huge block of cheese which always sat on the back counter of the shop quietly ageing. By the time our piece reached us it had oozed generously through a loose wrapping of greaseproof paper and was crazed with hard yellow cracks like a parched desert. There was no alternative but to toast it and for that slicing was necessary. It always resisted the best efforts of Mam whether she was armed with 'the big knife' or 'the little sharp knife' and provoked sharp and bitter comment when Mam took the weekly order to the shop. That is partly why I hated cheese and never touched it. I could never digest anything as cantankerous as that.

Because of 'the big knife', I thought it normal for slices of meat to have a rough sort of ploughed up texture to the surface. Regardless of the fact that this knife was useless for carving, Mam somehow hacked away at the Sunday joint, and we got strange thick woolly looking slices of meat with the odd bits and edges that defied the old saw blade.

Of course Mam's method of cooking did nothing to make the meat easier to slice. She never made any great claims to being a good cook, more a follower of the hit or miss school; the results of her culinary efforts varied between melt in the mouth and belt in the mouth. What with rationing and having to do the best you could with what you got, the Sunday roast was most unpredictable of all. Indeed, it was a rabbit more often that not, and stewed more often than roasted. (But I was strictly forbidden to tell anyone about that.)

We had a gas cooker which had yet to learn the discipline of regulating its temperature. You turned the tap on full to light it and get a good heat going, then turned the tap back to the first half or quarter turn to sustain the temperature you thought you might have reached, and just waited till the food was cooked. At this point it was quite usual to hear the shilling drop, and the gas went out.

Mam was never one to waste and recoiled from the idea of running anything at full power, so our oven rarely reached a temperature much above warm. Added to this frugality in the use of gas – 'another shilling in the meter we'll want before Monday if I don't watch it' – Mam had no patience with anything that didn't cook quickly, so she adapted the principles of roasting to her own nature. The joint went into the oven on Saturday morning with a milk pudding. After a quick half hour we had a gritty moist pudding for Saturday dinner and the joint was left to sit in its own perspiration till Sunday morning. It then had a seasonal fruit tart for company and a border of potatoes to roast. Any left over rice pudding went back in too and came out thick and tough enough to reinforce a bomb shelter.

When we had our plates in front of us, everything had such a thick overcoat of gravy, there was no way of telling whether the meat should have had more or less cooking. In charge of the Gas Board our Mam should have been – that would have cooked Hitler's goose or at least given it a nasty hot flush.

Sometimes I went to Granddad's 'down below' for Sunday dinner. By this I mean proper dinner, at mid-day. 'Lunch' was a snack one might have at mid-morning, fortification between an early breakfast and late dinner. We always called at Granddad's after church. Our house was at the top of the hill above town, and we walked down to the church almost at the bottom of the valley. At that time the post-war building of new homes had not begun, and we could walk down to the town, avoiding the streets taking the road which, though tarred, was little more than a lane with high banks and hedges where I could look forward to the flowers in season – celandines, violets, bluebells and dog roses. The road turned across the hill towards the town high street, skirting a low whitewashed farmhouse and a small wood which straddled the valley. If time was short, we cut down a path through the wood which brought us to the back gate of the church.

Grandad's house lay further along the road where it became the Avenue. The houses here were of stone and red brick, with long smooth front lawns and steps leading up to the front gates. The whole air of gentility was undisturbed by war, and Grandad's house, the smallest in the row, lay at the far end, like a full stop at the end of a pleasant conversation. Here, the avenue overlooked the school and the Miners' Welfare Institute which marked the start of the high street.

We usually met up with aunty Gwen and aunty Doreen at church, and then went back to their house. A cup of tea for Mam and Dad, and for me an inspection of the pop crate in the larder to make a choice of drink – lemonade, cherry, lime or, my favourite, dandelion and burdock. This was a taste later to be generally ousted by Coca Cola, but I have to this day stayed faithful to the memory of dandelion and burdock and do not care for Coke. Why go for fizzy water when you have a taste for champagne?

I was always pleased to be staying for Sunday dinner at Grandad's. Aunty Gwen and Doreen produced this between them. Doreen, tall, thin and quick on her feet, digging, cutting and picking the vegetables from the garden. Gwen, slow, soft spoken and portly, patiently scraping, peeling and chopping, then later Doreen taking over at the finish, organising the table and bringing the meal together. Their oven was heated from the coal fire which was always lit on Sunday mornings, no matter what privations of coal rationing might occur during the rest of the week.

There was a browning to the food and a crispness that I could actually smell, and the climax of this production was worth waiting for. Judging the moment, between the steaming, crackling, richly brown joint emerging from the oven, and the juice-rich gravy being placed on the table, Granddad took the long, smooth bladed carving knife from the drawer. The thin blade gleamed as Granddad ran his thumb along it, then flashed a warning as he flicked it rhythmically over the sharpening steel. There was, to me, so much more panache to this ritual than scraping a knife blade up the concrete wall. I was impressed, the warning not to touch because of the sharpness of the blade was quite unnecessary.

The joint of meat would then be delicately coaxed to yield wafer thin juicy slices which never needed chewing. And aunty Gwen always made very thin gravy revealing every morsel on the plate.

There was one thing that puzzled me though: I never saw a bread knife in Granddad's house. When I was there at teatime on occasion during the rest of the week, the carving knife was used on the bread. After a careful scrape with the minimum of margarine, sliver after sliver of wafer thin bread slices came off the loaf, a possible explanation of the parable concerning the couple of loaves feeding the five thousand. What they would have given for the extra luxury of a cucumber from Granddad's garden, also cut thin, like tissue paper!

I wonder if the chap who first introduced humankind to the ready-sliced loaf ever met my family?

A Proper Lady

'Don't put your finger up your nose – it's not ladylike.'

It was a haunting phrase which I heard so often as Mam anxiously guided me on the path to being a lady.

'Proper tomboy you are,' she would say in an effort to shame me into daintiness or gentility, though I took it as a compliment. If I was a tomboy, then I could compete with my peers and generally have more fun.

Ladies, on the other hand, did not come across as fun people at all. They always had clean socks and underwear; they might have darned and mended clothes, even displaying pride in the neatness of the repair, but they never sported holes in un-mended garments. Ladies wore their hair in tight rows of curls or ringlets, or cut ruler straight and kept tidy with a pristine bow of ribbon. They pulled their skirts down over their knees, sat up straight, never dragged their feet or scuffed their shoes, said please and thank you nicely, always carried a fresh handkerchief and never put fingers up their noses. Above all – no knicker leg ever hung down.

I was never aware of keenly wanting to emulate being a lady, but the image was always being thrust at me like an impossible goal, akin to seeking nirvana or the Holy Grail. Its constancy made it impossible to offend against it, so even if I was playing cricket, climbing a tree or taking a ride on a set of old pram wheels, I instinctively hitched up my socks, pulled down my skirt and checked that my hair ribbon was tightly in place. Any suspicion of a droop in the knicker department was hoisted firmly upward. Being a lady was hard work, and not likely to get any easier.

Mam managed to get hold of a nice bit of material. Brand new it was, tartan, and good enough to warrant a trip to Mrs Thomas the dressmaker.

Mrs Thomas lived in a row of cottages just outside town, a short terrace with each house having an identical tiny patch of grass between the stone wall fronting them all and the front door. All that was left now of the days of a busy open cast coal mine.

It was a long way to walk when I had to concentrate on keeping my hair tidy, my hands clean and my feet marching to the steady bump of my gas mask on my backside. Mam insisted on the gas mask, which usually stayed undisturbed at the bottom of the hall stand. I think it was because she was in slightly unfamiliar territory and possibly deep down felt that the Great German War Machine might consider Mrs Thomas' sewing machine a menacing threat to its victory. Who knew when the attack would come? So we took our gas masks.

Mrs Thomas was glad of the business anyway. After a bit of measuring there was a lot of 'oohing' and 'aahing' – 'lovely colour it is, enough for a big hem too, for growing. Sew up nice it will' – and by Easter I had a new skirt with pleats, buttons and, of course, a large hem to allow for growth.

News of the impending skirt had engendered enthusiasm for an 'ensemble', and aunty Gwen and Doreen did a bit of judicious unpicking of old jumpers and re-knitting. By the time my skirt was ready to wear, they were able to present me with a matching jumper plus a bolero top.

It's funny really, but perhaps because of shortages and rationing, although I enjoyed having new clothes, if there weren't any, it didn't bother me much.

Mam was over the moon; I was a little more pragmatic. New clothes – great. Parading around to be shown off while in constant fear of creasing, marking or in any way disturbing the 'haute couture' was not my idea of fun. Clothes would be worn, but not worn out or made shabby.

'Coupons,' said Mam tartly, 'won't stretch to new all the time.'

But Mam had really got the bit between her teeth this time.

'Ringlets,' she said thoughtfully.

It was Saturday evening and Mam was already thinking ahead to Sunday morning, Sunday best clothes and church. My heart sank.

I'd had a busy day. The entire morning had been taken up with helping aunty Gwen and aunty Doreen to decorate the church for Easter Sunday

was lost in the mists of chalk dust; Lydia's aggressive behaviour and attitude problems just kept reinforcing the policy of keeping her on the move. Besides, there were always the 'notes from mothers' which seemed to initiate a quick shift of place.

I came home from school that day to find Mam's arsenal all laid out – fine tooth comb, coal tar soap, liquid paraffin and old towels.

'The nit nurse wasn't at school today, was she?' asked Mam anxiously. I shook my head.

'We'd better get to work on them nits then, before she do come.'

My head was scrubbed, combed, scrubbed again and plastered with a paraffin mixture which stung my scalp and stank abominably, and then I had to suffer a timeless purgatory before it was washed off. Even after the final wash, the smell was pretty pungent. But I stuck it out grimly, glad of anything to rid me of those nasty little beasts that made my head itch so.

Next day, I was given a letter to hand to my teacher. Important stuff! I was always being given notes to hand to someone or other – the grocer, baker, butcher et al, but these were just pieces of paper folded over. The one I had to take to school was in an envelope, and stuck down too! This was like being entrusted with secret news about the war effort, and only I was responsible for making sure that it reached the right hands intact.

Actually, Miss Davies, when she opened the letter said nothing. She just gave a little sigh, glanced at my still greasy hair, put the letter aside and moved Lydia forward two rows.

The nit nurse didn't visit school till almost the end of term, and for the first time I felt real fear at the prospect of presenting myself for inspection. In the worst event, I could end up losing every strand of my hair and have to wear a woolly hat like Lydia. And I certainly did not have her fierce spirit and willingness to fight off the taunts and jibes. I would just have to run away, or kill myself, or…

I had submitted, and only cried once, to regular combing and stinking of paraffin, until Mam was satisfied that my head was clean again. But she wasn't a professional like the nit nurse. Suppose she had missed one of those horrible crawling and leaping creatures?

When my moment came, the nurse barely glanced at me and I was dismissed without comment, but a couple of days later Lydia turned up at school with the woolly hat sitting tightly on her scalp, fists and feet ready for anyone who dared question or snigger. There but for the grace of Mam and stinking paraffin...

My plaits were secure for a few years yet, right up to the time that the film 'South Pacific' hit the local cinema. The war had been over long enough for us to start romanticising about it, and with the story being set on a tropical island the cinema queue went right up the dark and winter cold high street every night of the week.

The star of the film, Mary Martin, sported a hairstyle which was immediately dubbed the 'Poodle Cut'. It was simply cut very short all over her head, but the concept of cutting hair in layers, and so short too, was quite outrageous at that time.

Mam hadn't seen the film but heard all about it.

'Daft! Real twp,' she said dismissively. This told me instantly that she had no romance in her soul. Me, I was hooked.

I saved my pocket money carefully over the following weeks, until I was ready to begin my scheme of Operation Hair Style.

Plaits were old fashioned. They didn't sit well under the Grammar School hat, and they quickly became straggly. I was always losing the end ribbons, and now that I had homework, the hair washing and drying were a real bind.

At first, Mam would only answer, 'Rubbish!' when I tendered any of these arguments, but I had the patience to wear her down, and at last we compromised.

My hair would be cut to shoulder length, nothing too grown up or glamorous, and then when I realised I didn't like it, I could let it grown again and Mam would be proved right all along. The clincher was that when my plaits were cut off, the local drama group wanted to borrow them for a production of an Ibsen play with all its Nordic characters. That appealed to Mam's sense of glory.

Mrs Evans, the ladies' side of Jones the Barber, was nervous when I turned up for my appointment.

'You sure it's a poodle cut you want? Ever so short it is. I can do a nice pageboy for you.'

I was nervous too; after all, I'd never been in the hairdresser's before, but my resolve (or my cussedness) was firming nicely with constant queries.

At last, Mrs Evans could procrastinate no longer, and out came the scissors. So different from uncle Bill's method! I could watch every move in the mirror as my hair was carefully divided, combed and snipped. Now I could appreciate the skill of styling and such visions of ultimate beauty danced in my head. After the pampering of washing, setting and drying with an actual hair drier, I was ready for the combing out. Cinderella? I was ready for the ball, and anything else life could throw at me.

I floated up the hill from town, light headed with pleasure, enjoying the glances of surprise, astonishment even, in the faces of people I met.

The euphoria lasted until I turned the final corner for home. Now I had to face Mam. She didn't shout.

'Oh Duw,' she whispered, 'what have you done? You didn't pay for that did you?!' Then there was a lot more mixed in with, 'hairdressers should have had more sense,' and how was I going to get my money back?

Finally, I crept off to bed before Dad came home, and got up for school the next morning as late as I dared. I clattered downstairs and suffered another restrained monotone tirade over a hurried breakfast.

At last I could escape to run for the bus, without even time to look in the mirror as I rammed my school hat on. But Mam wasn't finished, and I didn't even make it to the front gate. 'Come back here quick,' she ordered in her best not-to-be-disobeyed voice!

'Now put this scarf over your head under your school hat.'

Then, her voice rising in panic, 'People will think you've got nits!'

A Town and Country Girl

One of the first signs that confirmed that the war was over was the sudden appearance of street lighting. The hand torch was no longer vital after daylight hours, necessary perhaps but not vital.

The gas lamps spaced along the streets reflected a gently flickering bluish glow over each small patch of road and pavement within its circle of light, and now that we could flash our torches un-shaded with the wartime regulation sticky paper, the night seemed as bright as day. We could walk confidently without reliance on familiar markers to touch, without fumbling for gate latches or groping for steps.

On the old iron lamp posts, the short cross bar under the light was an invitation for creating a swing with a piece of rope, regardless of whether it was daylight or not.

But this was not to last for long. Before we knew what was happening, the old graceful iron lamp posts were dismantled and rough grey concrete ones put in their place. Then suddenly, the whole town was ablaze with electric light and we could see from our house right across the green to the houses on the other side.

Most important of all, the shadows were penetrated sufficiently that we no longer had to advance slowly and cautiously upon the outside lavatory.

I was telling Marjorie all about our lighting. We were staying with aunty Doll in Herefordshire, which was our annual holiday. Marjorie lived in the same village and although we only met up once a year, she was definitely on my list of six best friends.

My tale of light and sweetness did not produce the expected reaction of envy and awe. In fact we had a fight when Marjorie call me a snob, and most contemptuous of all, a real town girl, a coded expression to describe someone who was pretty stupid about the realities of life, like hay making or skinning a rabbit.

I made a dignified exit from this tirade by sticking out my tongue and flouncing off. Then I kicked stones all the way up the sandy lane to aunty Doll's house.

I went through the gate in the back wall to the orchard where I settled comfortably in the summer scented grasses to ponder the accusations flung at me. World War Two might be over, but this personal one had a lot of negotiation to run to prevent hostilities breaking out again.

Was I town or country? Which did I want to be anyway? Marjorie was nearly a year older than I and so confident in her environment that I had come to accept that country life was superior to town life. Now it was time to do a little evaluation.

As I sat under an apple tree and pondered upon the question, I soon came to the conclusion that I could not be categorised. Sure, where I lived we had more than one street and numbered houses which was alien to this village, but in summer when the council came to cut the grass on the green, we had glorious days of hay making, when games had a serious purpose. We were 'helping' the council, even if they didn't see it that way.

Just as at aunty Doll's, we lived on vegetables from the garden, though we didn't have as many fruit bushes, nor an orchard, and Dad didn't make cider like uncle Will did.

Ah yes! Cider. Now that was a country secret. I knew they made it from apples, and even talking about it left Mam torn between muttering dire warnings of eternal damnation and giggling. When we stayed with aunty Doll, uncle Will would come into the kitchen with a jug of cider to go on the supper table just as I and my cousins were going off to bed. After that, the cider seemed to induce vague giggling and laughter that lulled me to sleep. No doubt about it, cider was a country mystery to me.

Pondering these mysteries was hungry work, and surely here in the orchard I'd be able to find something to eat. The nuts weren't ready yet and the plums and blackberries were still green. It looked like apples again then, as long as I could remember which tree yielded the sweet eating apples as opposed to the tart green cookers.

For a moment I was quite homesick for my hometown. The strawberries and raspberries would be ripe in the garden now, and if I'd been 'up top' at Gran's house, she might have sent me to look for an egg in the nesting boxes while she cut a thick slice of home cured bacon in anticipation of supper or breakfast.

But of course, I had the townie sophistication that comes with travel. With Mam and Dad, I had been on three buses and a train to get to this village, and even if one sneered at townies generally, that had to count for something. Marjorie had never been on a train, her furthest adventure being a rare trip on the bus to Hereford, (change at Leominster). One up to me. However, she could leap up and ride on tractors to the manner born, while I was forbidden to go anywhere near the muddy things for fear of messing up my clothes.

Mam interrupted my thoughts.

'There you are then. Mind you haven't been sitting on anything muddy. I want you to go down the Post Office and fetch a bucket of drinking water.'

I went off on my errand with more food for thought. I reckoned it was a sign of a sophisticated townie to live in a house with running water on tap indoors, cold and hot (if the fire was going). We had a bathroom upstairs as well. My country friend, Marjorie, had nothing like that. Just like aunty Doll's cottage, Marjorie's home had a large water butt at the side of the house which collected rainwater for washing and cleaning. The bath hung on a nail in the yard. The Post Office, at the bottom of the lane, had a pump at the side of the building which pumped up clear spring water for drinking for anyone who wanted or had to fetch it. It was a marker stage in childhood to be regarded as big and strong enough for the job of water carrying. Some thought it a sign of status, I definitely considered it to be a pain in the day.

When I clanked up to the pump, Marjorie was already there, half hidden by a vigorously growing pear tree trained against the side wall of the Post Office.

She glanced at me sideways, then concentrated on her task of working the pump. Apparently addressing the bucket like a go-between, she said casually, 'Goin' swimming after dinner. You comin'?' Taking over the pump handle, in turn I addressed the flow of water into the bucket.

'Yeh O.K. See you by the bridge then!'

It had taken a lot of patience for aunty Doll to convince Mam that the shallow stream, rushing and shushing over its sandy bed strewn with pebbles and stones, was quite safe for paddling, being only inches deep.

I loved it. Denied the pleasures of the seaside all through my early childhood, because of distance and hostilities, the joy of splashing about in water was a rare treat. Marjorie and I would go as often as we could to lie on our stomachs, waving arms and legs about, quite convinced that we were swimming.

It was a perfect afternoon, hot and sunny with just the gentle gurgle of the stream washing its stones. Even the languid cows in the fields on either side chewed the grass silently. We swam the English Channel, or probably further, several times, until hunger and a lowering sun reminded us that suppertime was not far off.

Sated with pleasure, refreshed and at peace with the world, we sauntered back along the river bank, flicking willow sticks through the nettles that dared to invade the path now and then and picking choice bunches of wide-eyed dog daisies. Once over the warm stone bridge we reached the parting of the ways.

'See you after?' I called as Marjorie turned towards home.

'Gorra do things after supper,' she replied, and hurried off.

Of course, I'd forgotten. Marjorie wasn't allowed out after daylight faded. When night came, it possessed the land. Houses were accustomed to shutting their light in and there wasn't a street lamp to be seen before the outskirts of Leominster, several miles away.

For Marjorie this meant jobs to be done indoors, no swings on the lamp post, no hide and seek in the sharp light and shadows, and certainly no evenings at friends' houses – they were too scattered.

I was content with the day. I no longer felt somehow inferior and neither did I feel the need to define myself as 'town' or 'country'. Each environment I experienced offered me much of itself and I was happy with what I had of both.

A Bit of Luck

Christmas had come and gone leaving the winter to drag slowly through its tired end towards spring.

I'd been having a great time playing in the snow with all the kids in the street, even being allowed a slide in the old pram, minus its wheels, that Tommy and Cliffie had acquired. Crossing the vast snowy wastes, my sleigh gliding like the wind across the icy surfaces, and calling my reindeer team to obey my commands, was quite tiring by the time I had reached Mrs Crisp's house, four doors up the street, so I went in a bit early for my tea.

The house was very quiet.

'Hush!' said Mam in a whisper, from where she sat hunched over the kitchen table. She and Mrs Sharp had clearly been enjoying a customary cup of tea or three, but now they were crouching over the tea cups as if waiting for a genie to appear.

Mrs Sharp slowly tilted an empty cup in its saucer. She lowered her voice in respect to the drama that was beginning to reveal itself as she gazed at the tea leaves.

'A tall dark stranger, yes – and a present, money I think.'

Mam was spellbound. I went to fetch my book. I'd heard it all before, at least twice a week and occasionally 'up top' at Gran's when Miss Evans the Milk came to call. Mam always lapped it up (the drama that is, not the milk) like a cat at the cream, and could always quote chapter and verse for its veracity, from an unexpected bill turning up to finding sixpence in the street.

Perhaps in spite of or because of the tea leaves, the week had started well, deceptively so as things turned out.

The start of the week had, in fact, been great; it was after all my birthday.

Since I'd been born just before the outbreak of World War Two, with its inevitable shortages of goods and food, I'd never been aware that to enjoy a birthday party it was necessary to have ice cream, balloons, cream cakes and all the trimmings we have since those times taken for granted. Then, a party was an occasion when ingenuity, surprise and initiative all came together to crown anticipation. Now that was excitement!

I felt a tremendous sense of thrill and status when I discovered that Mam could not only produce a jelly for my party, but a tin of fruit as well!

Much of the rest of the food was a matter of mystery and conjecture as my guests turned up, with perhaps a small pack of sandwiches here, a pot of paste or a bag of Welsh cakes there – all put together to make a fabulous spread with its centrepiece of tinned fruit and jelly. Every crumb would be devoured before the rounds of party games – Squeak Piggy Squeak, Pass the Parcel, Hide and Seek – on and on to exhaustion.

The tiny maggot of misfortune began to wriggle as I opened my presents. Amid the books, puzzles and hand made toys, was a knitted shoulder bag from aunty Doll.

Now I thought the multi-coloured wool and fold over flap with its large 'real gold' button presented a very chic effect, but Mam went straight to the inside, fingers searching and prodding every inch of lining. Reluctantly she handed it back.

'Very unlucky that,' she said, in a voice heavy with foreboding. I was mystified, even when I had some sort of explanation.

'Giving a bag empty brings bad luck. Should be a half penny in it. Then you'll always have money.'

Mam clearly saw a future of unrelenting poverty for me as a direct result of aunty Doll's oversight. A long time afterwards I realised I should have gone out and found a four leaf clover, two magpies or a black cat to redress the balance, but I didn't. I went on to compound my misfortune.

The next morning I sat down to breakfast only for Mam to discover that I'd shuffled my cutlery so that the knives were crossed. Inevitably there'd be a row in the house before sunset. Then in attempting to put thing right, a knife clattered to the floor.

Oh calamity! That meant a man would knock on the door before the day was much older. A fork wouldn't have been so bad. That would have changed the caller's sex, and hardly a day passed without one of the neighbouring housewives popping in for a chat or 'can you borrow me a bit of sugar' – or coal or tea or whatever. A male caller however could mean the rent man, the insurance man or someone selling something. No matter how you looked at it, it was probably going to cost money, except for the vicar calling, so Mam would have to give everything an extra bit of spit and polish just in case.

Now the arrival of the rent man or insurance man could always be calculated, but there were other who presented a different problem. These were the hawkers of goods, services or salvation. The trouble was that Mam could very rarely say 'No.' She didn't mind the 'Shoni onion' man with his festoons of onions draped all over his bicycle, because onions were a staple part of every dinner and Dad was hard put to grow enough.

It was the others with the 'gift of the gab' that Mam fell easy prey to, and the ones she actually feared were the Sheikh sellers, as she called them, with their so alien looking turbans and large suitcases.

Mam always had an eye to the window to 'see who was about,' and if she saw some peddler lugging a suitcase beginning his patient plod around the circle, she took immediate action. First I would have to be hauled to safety (saved from white slavery perhaps, or a least from the Evil Eye). Not that I knew anything about such things. One minute I was playing outside, hardly aware of the stranger with his large pack of mystery, beginning his weary trudge from door to door. Then in an instant I was yanked indoors, sat in the back room behind closed curtains and hissed at to be silent and still in the one command – 'Look quiet now!' Come to think of it, in another time, Mam could have been a highly successful hostage taker.

Mam picked up my knife from the floor, 'I just hope it won't be anybody selling something, that's all,' she said, looking at me with a hint of threat or perhaps warning in her voice. I hoped so too. I had a feeling that Mam's expectation was clearly contrary to her hopes, and I had a nasty feeling that one way or another, I would be paying the price for the triumph of expectation.

When the knock came, it took Mam by surprise. It was early evening. Dad was home from work, but was busy digging in the garden. Therefore Mam was a pushover, and the smartly dressed young salesman was over the step and in the front door before Mam could get her pinny off. She had lost the high ground and was left in a position of weak defence. She was also tired, it being a Wednesday when she gave the bedrooms their weekly 'good do'. She'd had carpets and rugs out on the washing line for a good beating, crawled under each bed in pursuit of fluff, polished everything that couldn't be moved and washed everything that could. It was a perfect set for the salesman and his vacuum cleaner.

He made great play of not finding any dust, and in the manner of the best stage magician, he scattered his own carefully prepared dirt on Mam's best front room carpet. With superb timing he spirited it away into his machine before Mam could fire off on both barrels. He then went on into the hall and halfway up the stairs.

Mam was impressed, I could see that, especially with the memory of all that brushing and carpet beating still fresh in her mind – and arms and back and legs. It was a pushover. A deal was made without troubling Dad to come in from the garden and express an opinion.

The funny thing was, Mam couldn't get on with that machine. In the first place, she couldn't accept that a piece of machinery could do any household task better than she could do it herself. Secondly, she was convinced that if the job didn't leave her worn out or at least puffed, then it hadn't been done properly. Actually, in this case, a week's evidence of dust and fluff gleaned after following the trail of the vacuum cleaner with a dust pan and brush, proved Mam's case to her satisfaction.

Not quite that simple though. Dad had a look at the infernal machine and pointed out that it was a bit unfair to condemn the cleaner so completely when all the time she'd had the hose plugged into the 'blow' end rather than the 'suck'. And anyway, they couldn't get their money back.

Mam had an answer though which loaded the whole sequence of events on to me.

'I told you not to fall your knife on the floor.'

The Barry Island Special

In my childhood world, 'luxury' was not a familiar word. In those days of the war years, it was not a word that was used at all. If the conversations around me were ever in danger of turning towards an idea that might be construed as wasteful, frivolous or downright luxurious, there were several tried and true conversation stoppers. The most common two I remember were either, 'Don't you know there's a war on?' or 'It's off for the duration'. I had no idea what the latter phrase meant, except that it must allude to some kind of holy ritual which was a killer of fun.

'Coach' was something to do with horses and no one had yet thought of harnessing the two words together to produce a new concept in travel.

The end of World War Two brought one luxury into my life which could not be scuppered by the 'Duration.' It was a trip on the Special Bus, the forerunner of the luxury coach. This was a vehicle ordered from the West Mon Bus Company, just for our street. There would be no disappointment of being left standing at the bus stop as a fully loaded bus trundled by on its way to where you wanted to go, leaving you thwarted and frustrated where you were already at. No rushing late to the bus stop to find that the bus had left early, or standing extra minutes in spiteful rain when the bus came late.

The Special Bus would come to our order, right to the door (or the street anyway) at the time we ordered it, and it would proclaim this to the world as it bore us away, with that one word on the front – Special.

The arrangements were started months ahead with many consultations over back garden fences, the nearest our little community ever came to a committee meeting.

I usually just got wind of the event from one of the other kids in the street, and would promptly run home to ask Mam if it was true – were we really going to the seaside on the last Saturday in July? There were no secrets on our patch.

There was much pursing of the lips and tutting about the price – 5 shillings each and half price for children, but we had to have a full bus mind. Somehow we filled the bus every year, I can never remember any family backing out or failing to pay up once committed. Finding the money each week must have been specially hard for the one or two families for whom the day trip to Barry Island constituted their annual holiday.

Mam even tried to conscript Gran. 'Ych I'm not going on no charrybang. Mrs Evans the Milk went on one once and was sick all the way home.'

I had to ask my teacher at school in order to discover that a charrybang was a charabanc, but it still didn't throw much light on the matter. To Mam and Gran the Special Bus was a charrybang.

The weeks dragged on in a fret of waiting, when Mam would often give me a screw of newspaper containing a weight of coins, telling me to run up the road and give the bundle to Mrs Crisp – and don't loiter or walk in the gutter, oh and make sure you see her write it down. I don't know why we had all the fuss and waiting on tenterhooks before the bus was irrevocably ordered. Everybody in the street always went on the summer outing, except for the Bowens who never socialised with anyone, otherwise the neighbours would think you couldn't afford it and there'd be all sorts of talk. So you bit the bullet and saved hard.

Now I could boast and swagger a bit at school. Of course, every street in my small Welsh mining town had its summer day trip, but ours was undoubtedly superior. Bevan Crescent going to Porthcawl? Well, we were going to Barry Island, which everyone knew had the best and biggest fun fair, and that you could get toffee apples and rock with writing all the way through each stick, and the clincher – all the barbed wire was gone from the beach and there were no roped off areas.

Nearer the day came the problem of what to wear. When childhood, a time of rapid physical growth, coincided with six years of war engendering clothing coupons and shortages of material, plus a tight family economy, the wardrobe was not extensive. There was my polka dot muslin which had come in a parcel from America, and I was lucky enough to be the only one in the family that it fitted. But that was out. By parental decree, that dress was my absolute best, for church on Sundays only. I didn't feel much enthusiasm for the parachute nylon dress aunty Doll had made for me; quite honestly it still felt like I was wearing a parachute, and I was nervous on windy days. In the end, it was decided it would have to be my 'decent' dress, the second best one, suitable for school and social visiting, and not yet relegated to 'old, for playing in!'

I knew though that I'd have to wear a cardigan and keep my liberty bodice on, because even if it was high summer, as Mam was so often heard to remark darkly, 'You never know.' She was also sure that once we had left the protection of the narrow valleys, the climate would be different. No doubt that's why Dad would be wearing his suit, like all the other men, and Mam would carry a coat over her arm.

Next, I just had to have a bathing costume. No problem. Aunty Gwen would knit me one in plenty of time. Then the 'piéce de resistance' – Grandad came up with an old car tyre inner tube, already inflated at the garage, so my safety from drowning was assured.

The week before the outing, when the 'pop' man called, we ordered extra. Normally we had a regular order for three bottles of pop a week, which Mam decided was enough to satisfy the family's boozing capacity, but on this special week we had two extra bottles to take with us, a dandelion and burdock and an ice cream soda. All the bottles had those lovely spring loaded clip on stoppers which popped so explosively when opened – especially after a shaking in the bus.

Almost there now. All that remained was to accept being sent to bed too early to sleep the night before the outing, and then to be chivvied out of bed when it was too early to wake up.

An extra scrubbing preceded a check for clean underwear, because 'you never know', then the top dressing was completed with a lecture about keeping clean and tidy till the bus came. Not easy in my second best frock and Sunday sandals. It limited my waiting time activities.

There was much scurrying about before we left to make sure the house was clean, and then there were sandwiches to cut and Welsh cakes to pack in a tin. The sandwiches were always a choice between fish paste or jam, always thick and very dry in spite of being tightly wrapped in brown paper bags, or (if you wished to demonstrate social superiority) greaseproof paper bought special. But who cared? Food eaten away from the table was the stuff of adventurers and explorers, with a heady flavour all of its own.

I watched at the window for an eternity until the bus turned into our street. I swelled with pride to see the magical words 'Special Bus' displayed above the driver's windscreen. It meant us. We were special. The bus was ours for the whole day, at our command to come and go as we ordered, and denied to the rest of the hoi polloi at every bus stop we passed.

Between eternal watches, I had trotted at intervals up to the corner, listening for the first sound of the bus straining up the hill. In the event, it arrived quite suddenly, turning the corner and catching me unawares.

Then came the really big moment. Which house would the driver choose to stop right outside? To have the 'Special Bus' stop right outside your house beat being milk monitor or winning at cricket. This was being Mohammed as the mountain rolled to a stop with a submissive rumble before you.

The scramble for seats was pretty important too. A window seat was not only good for seeing, but for being seen too, as some evidence of the tales of adventure we would relish and embellish in the telling at school the next term. Gradually the rest of the bits and pieces of families with bags, brollies and raincoats climbed aboard, dads in suits and best shoes, mams in second best dresses and no hats. Dad saw to the stowing of my car tube at the back of the bus, which involved a lot of pushing and shoving and general consultation.

The door was shut, the windows were opened, the sun shone with a steady glow and we were off – well almost. Mrs Evans was sure she'd forgotten to lock her back door and Mam had to go back for the tin of Welsh cakes left on the kitchen table. Couldn't go without that. Every mam and aunty had an inexhaustible supply of Welsh cakes to pass up and down the aisles both going and coming back, and all along the beach. We could never be sure, once we had left the protection of the valley for the land beyond, that we wouldn't starve to death before supplies reached us.

My car inner tube, still inflated, took up a lot of room, and I was a bit self conscious about it by this time, but my painted paint tin, for making sand castles, was as good as anyone's. Better. Mine was painted a brilliant green inside and out. Surprisingly, perhaps, the actual journey didn't mean very much; I so wanted to be there, at Barry Island. I wasn't greatly into staring at the scenery, being more inclined to look out for the next bus queue so I could look down my nose at it as we swept past, whilst wallowing in the luxury of a padded seat of dark red moquette instead of having to bear the bone juddering wooden slats of the normal service buses.

Mrs Evans was determined that we should all sing. Up and down the aisle she went, giving her attention and encouragement to anyone not giving enthusiastic voice. Familiar hymn tunes, Cwm Rhondda, Roll out the Barrel – no one could plead ignorance of words or tune. Mam moved her lips and stretched a bit of a smile across her teeth. Her sausage curls were unused to such liberty from curlers and mob cap in the morning and she didn't want to crease anything before we arrived. She'd be singing with the best of them on the way back though.

We had barely left the valley before the first tin of Welsh Cakes was passed along the bus. Mam always thought it a bit pushy to be first, but then 'that was Mrs Williams for you' she muttered. The mams, grans and aunties all had their fears of mass starvation allayed by the time the first cry went up – The Sea! We were so stuffed full of Welsh Cakes by that time that we were in far greater danger of sinking like heavy dough the minute we entered the water.

I can still remember that first feel of the sand to feet which were always enclosed in ankle socks and shoes and used to tarmac or grass for playing on. The beach sand was a completely new experience of warm yielding softness. I was never allowed to leave off my socks, even in the normal routine of play and going to school. It was, I think, more a way of measuring poverty, or an inability to deal with it, to be seen without socks or proper shoes. The only compromise was a pair of new leather sandals bought each summer ready for and worn for the first time on the Sunday School Whitsun march.

Now, like the rest of the kids, I wanted to jump and roll and laugh out loud for the sheer joy of the feeling of freedom and the softness between my toes. Even the mams and aunties giggled and called to each other and became quite skittish, not even noticing the protective cardigans, jumpers and vests being abandoned by the young ones. This older generation must have viewed the beach with different eyes; the grim rusty coils of barbed wire swept away, gun batteries dismantled, and there was freedom to walk on their own shores with their men.

Before we went into the water, we had to have another Welsh Cake each to keep up our strength. Everyone had been made fully aware that if you ate a meal before you went into the water, you would get the cramp and die most likely. As long as we didn't spend too long in the water, the last Welsh Cake should just about carry us through to dinner time. Lunch was unheard of. We always had our dinner at midday – a good solid meal to go back to work on.

My car tube made me quite popular. I marched out with the other kids to chase the receding tide and bravely launched my doughty vessel, with myself aboard, in ankle deep water. This was the moment of bravado and whistling in the wind. All those tales at school of how far and fast each could swim, the confidence, the boasting, were the stuff of dreams when faced with this endless expanse of cold, grey, unfamiliar water. Some would cheat, flailing about with one foot on the bottom, while a few would wade out bravely, standing waist deep, and explain later how they would have gone so much further if not sternly recalled by one of the duty mams or dads dipping their feet at the water's edge.

Here, dresses were daintily tucked into knicker legs that had proper elastic, or held coyly at knee level, whilst the men, free of their heavy best jackets, collars and ties, rolled their trouser legs as high as they would go and hooked thumbs into braces. It was a scene of complete abandonment.

At this point I discovered that a woolly knitted bathing costume was about as much use as a sponge mackintosh. The water-logged wool immediately stretched, pulling the crutch down to my knees and elongating the shoulder straps to several times their original length. Even after I had been given a discreet wring out and the straps knotted up somewhere around my ears, the walk back up the beach was quite a drag. Fortunately there was plenty of car tube to preserve my modesty and dignity.

The sandwiches lived up to their name. Plastic containers had yet to be dreamed up; we had to do our best with paper bags, tins, baskets and the shopping frail. (The frail? – great granny to a plastic carrier bag fashioned from any fabric from oil cloth to old curtains, though the fashion that year was for raffia covered cardboard milk bottle tops stitched together into the required shape). None of the packaging was any match for the combination of wind and sand at Barry Island, or for our forgetfulness of being in an alien environment and neglecting to brush our fingers before eating. But even the grittiness in the teeth couldn't spoil the picnic with its freedom of not having to mind your manners or eat-up-all-your-greens-or-you-wont-get-any-pudding. The fish paste and jam were gourmet delights.

The climax of the afternoon was going up the shows. 'Fun fair' was not a title we generally used, and by today's standards would have been too grand a description for the patchy arrangement of showtime and rattling equipment put back together after the suspension of fun 'for the duration'. A bit like unpacking long stored favourite clothes, only to find the odd moth hole here and there.

Sweets were still on ration, but we managed to find toffee apples and popcorn to fortify ourselves for the sedately galloping wooden horses and the water chute, before the squealing fright of the ghost train and the caterpillar which hurled us around, dipping and rising crazily until we shrieked for mercy. It was thrill upon thrill until we could take no more.

The faithful 'Special Bus' bore the day stoically. As others came and went to timetables, it stood quiet at the end of the headland road, facing out to sea and perhaps wondering to itself about boats. It wasn't forgotten by us during the day though, not by a long chalk. In meeting up with other kids on the beach we would point out the bus with casual pride, especially if they had come by train or service bus from Cardiff.

'Come on the 'Special Bus' we did. Up there look. The dark red one with posh seats.'

How naturally the snobbishness of social climbing comes, even to the young, especially those accustomed to walking wherever a bus fare could be saved.

The homeward journey was enlivened by the singing of those old enough to stay awake. I hovered between dreaming and the day's vivid memories, through the opening choruses of hymns (well it was nearly Sunday), and Sospan Fach, to the more interesting and novel ditties where words were left out or drowned in giggles. Mrs Morgan even did a little jig in the aisle, her hair all unpinned and her blouse straining to break free of her skirt. Once or twice, a sharp corner or piece of rough road sent her sprawling across someone else, her shrieks of laughter coming from a face still glowing with the heat of the sun now cooled beneath the horizon.

Even Mam was so uncustomarily relaxed that her face was folded in a permanent smile. She even let out a little giggle now and then, and for one horrified second I had a vision of her joining in the dance with Mrs Morgan. It was entertaining and amusing for someone else's mam, to show herself off like that – but your own! It didn't bear thinking about.

Stopping for a quick drink was out of the question. Even at my tender age, though not really aware of the Welsh 'dry' Sunday, I was beginning to cotton on vaguely to some sort of social conduct that existed apropos drinking.

Ladies didn't drink anything in public, except for tea of course, and never touched beer anyway (or so they declared), but would toy with a glass of port at Christmas, weddings and funerals. Since none of these occasions were part of the 'Special Bus' outing, ladies stuck with the last of the dandelion and burdock in enamel mugs, all part of the day's general abandoned behaviour. The men stuck it out with great fortitude – dandelion and burdock for the goose, dandelion and burdock for the gander, but a furtive check on the time comforted them that we would be back well before closing time at the Workman's Club.

Before the valleys closed in on us again, there was a collection for the driver effected with the aid of Mr Evan's cap. The driver after all was working and doing a stalwart task, kindly consenting to drop people on minor detours (the men mostly) at every corner next to a Workman's Club, that cherished institution where the ale could legally be drawn on a Sunday.

I was asleep before the bus turned the last corner, its revving roar a lullaby to a small body awash with dreams of space, water, sun and freedom.

Next week, I shall be boarding a plane to fly to another country in far less time than it took our 'Special Bus' to reach the seaside. I know and fully accept that travel broadens the mind, and I look forward to my trip, but if only I could experience this journey with the mind of that long ago child of a so-called deprived generation, born into the limits and restrictions of a war time era.

The 'Special Bus' really was a magic ride that opened up our lives spent in the Valleys, bringing us to new experiences of all our senses. It told us that the world didn't end at Cardiff. Sitting on the beach at Barry Island, gazing at the great expanse of sea that went on till it met the sky, I for one knew that there was an undreamed of, unexplored world out there, and this was my finest conception of it.

Deep and Crisp and Fever

Christmas began straight after Bonfire Night. During the war years, it would be an exaggeration to call Bonfire Night a low key affair; there were no bonfires or fireworks for fear of them being seen from the air, and for the same reason all windows were tightly blacked out after dark. A few sparklers set off round the living room fire with the centre light switched off was the high spot of the evening.

Even when life moved on into peacetime, Guy Fawkes was usually only remembered in a few sparklers waved about, outside now, round a very meagre bonfire; coal was still scarce, and anything that made fuel for home heating was carefully hoarded, not wasted on the frivolity of a bonfire.

So with the kindling of excitement carefully laid but not yet ignited, we began the build up to Christmas early in November.

Rationing was still in operation, and though the Government was gradually easing the strictures, we didn't. As Mam also said darkly when she stored away anything that was spare, 'You never know.' And I never did.

If anything, we tightened our belts a little more so we could save our ration coupons for extras at Christmas.

Ever the optimist, Mam put a tin of fruit on her weekly grocery order – nothing specific, just fruit. To stipulate size and variety was pointless anyway, and we were always thrilled with whatever we got – if we received anything at all. This was never delivered with the order; it was much too valuable for that. Mam would go down to town on a Saturday, and at the grocers would enter into a low tone conversation with Mr Pegler, the manager. His side of it was pretty brief; he either had nothing, or he had one small consignment of large peaches, small pears or whatever – take it or leave it. Mam always took it, quickly and deftly hidden at the bottom of her shopping basket, while I hoped and crossed my fingers that it was of the most exotic variety that only grew in tropical climes. Just knowing that there would be a tin of fruit (in syrup, too), safely stowed away under the bed in the back bedroom, had all the excitement of doing something ever so slightly illegal and getting away with it, adding a little extra flavour to the feast at teatime on Christmas Day. I think Mam got some extra 'buzz' too if she heard Mrs Smith the Corner complaining that there wasn't a tin of fruit to be had in town.

In my comics, the characters always tucked into turkey at Christmas, a stranger and monster bird as alien to me as stewed ostrich. Since chicken only appeared on dinner tables at Christmas time if you were lucky, this was far more special. During the leanest years of the war, Mam eked out the chicken by mixing in a little rabbit meat. This was sent to us by aunty Doll from Herefordshire. It had been shot by uncle Bill, had a label tied round its neck and was dispatched to us totally unwrapped – a wise precaution for a time when post could be delayed by rail diversions and air raids for days. The postman always delivered this with his nose and the rabbit kept as far from each other as possible. Sometimes the postal delays were over lengthy, and Mam dumped the rabbit at the bottom of the garden for Dad to bury under the rhubarb.

Small wonder then that I disliked rabbit meat intensely, so every helping of roast meat or cold meat sandwiches was chicken for me, or so Mam assured me. It was amazing how much meat you could get off one small chicken – I must have eaten a chicken and a half all by myself.

The first years of peace were bound to be extra special. We could buy things without counting the coupons, plan, put up lights, and Santa Claus could ride the skies without fear of being shot down. As peace gathered momentum, at last we stood in a blaze of light under the stars around the bonfire on November 5th at the back of the scout hut. The exploding colours of rockets, thunderflashes and Catherine Wheels whirled and streaked above our heads like low shooting stars and we warmed ourselves on scorched potatoes seasoned with the stuff of dreams and imagination. What an entrance to the winter season!

This, too, was the year that the snow came early. After days of freezing rain followed by hard frosts, overnight the wind whipped up great swirls of frozen meringue and piled them along the front of the house. In the morning, while a featherbed sky promised more of the same and Dad struggled round the side of the house to dig a passageway from the road to the front door, I climbed out of the bedroom window and slid down the drift of snow, over the top of the hedge to the middle of the road. Now I could identify with the antics I followed in the Beano comic! (Except, I couldn't help thinking, that none of the Beano characters seemed to suffer a chafed and frozen backside when they cavorted in the snow.)

There followed magic days. Even the schools were closed. They'd stayed open all through the threats of bombing and wartime shortages, but the snow defeated them. Instead, we turned to winter sports. A wealth of ingenuity in the neighbourhood adapted pram wheel bases and boxes to sleds, trays to toboggans and old cricket bats to skis.

I came home from the Showfield with its Swiss mountain pistes and multiple cresta runs earlier than the other kids. For once I was feeling tired and was unusually aware of the cold.

Mam pulled off my boots, felt my hands and face and packed me off to bed with a bowl of onion soup. I didn't argue; a good sleep seemed a very attractive idea.

At intervals, faces appeared and voices murmured, but I slept well on into the next day. I still had no inclination to get out of bed, although I was more alert when I heard Dr McKay's voice at the bottom of the stairs. His approach up the stairs and across the landing was slow and measured. I didn't wonder at that, since the incident of his last visit.

The year before, Mam had not been well and Dad insisted on calling Dr McKay. After making sure that the house was clean and there was a fresh towel in the bathroom, Mam had scurried back to bed just before the doctor arrived.

'Nothing Serious,' was his verdict, but he lectured on about 'a tonic' and not doing so much, resting and not getting so obsessed with all this polishing and dusting. He would be back at the end of the week.

Of course, when he left Mam ignored his advice completely and carried on with her normal routine. She did take the medicine though. Mam was a great believer in 'a pill for every ill' and we had a bulging cupboard to prove it.

The routine was as before for the doctor's next visit, with Mam 'resting' in bed. He seemed quite satisfied with her state of health and hurried across the landing to wash his hands in the bathroom before leaving.

There was an almighty crash. Mam dashed from the bedroom to find Dr McKay sprawled across the landing floor with the rug wedged under the bath. The bare, brilliantly gleaming lino gave mute evidence of Mam's polishing, and, with the doctor's glare of accusation flashing from Mam's guilt ridden face to the lino, there was no need for words. Dr McKay gathered his dignity, black homburg and black bag and left.

This was the first visit since then. He seemed quite relieved to have made it to my bedroom and to be standing on a carpet. Dr McKay was never a man to waste words; he blamed my feverishness on the unusual excitement of the winter sports coupled with the fact that I was growing quickly and probably just 'outgrowing my strength.' Another week off school and I would be fine.

And so it was, although it was an unusual first term at the Grammar School, the snow was still with us, though great swathes had been cut through it. The buses around our streets trundled along giant passageways in the high banked drifts, but the town at the bottom of the valley was reasonable clear. As we disembarked from the school bus at Maes-y-Cwmmer, we had a clear path down to the river, then the walk up the mountain at the other side still had plenty of bright clean snow. It was too steep for buses to get up that road at any time, and the other traffic wasn't bothering to try.

I loved being back at school. The build up to Christmas was beginning and the talk was of parties and new clothes, even of party dresses. A special dress ('dress' was so much more sophisticated than 'frock') just for a party. Now that really was an exciting novelty!

I could boast that I had been allowed to choose some material from Jones and Richards, maroon taffeta it was, and vastly superior to anything obtained by some of my class mates from the Bargoed Emporium.

I knew exactly how I wanted my dress to look. I'd seen it in a Hollywood film. Apart from the full swirling skirt and nipped in waist, the most important feature to me was the 'sweetheart' neckline, something which didn't button tightly round my throat, but curved modestly below my collarbone.

I wanted so much to be back at school that I ignored my flagging energy levels and the fact that most of my efforts were below par. Then one morning I fainted during School Assembly and was packed off home.

Dr McKay ordered more rest, and a week in bed. I don't know whether I suffered more from my physical symptoms, a complete lack of energy and enthusiasm for anything, or the bitter disappointment of missing the school parties. To make things worse, aunty Doll had created and dispatched my party dress to arrive in plenty of time, and I discovered that Mam had elaborated on my instructions for a 'sweetheart' neckline. She wanted to be sure it would cover my chest well so I wouldn't catch cold. Taffeta dresses in December indeed! The result was a neckline that curved nearer my tonsils than my heart and I hated it. It was little consolation that I wouldn't be wearing it anyway.

And so Christmas approached in a lacklustre way. Even the still lingering deep snow drifts had lost much of their charm. The snow was slowly becoming wetter and dirtier whilst restricting our movements and activities, and it was often overlaid with the grey winter fog creeping up the valleys.

In spite of war and weather, Christmas Eve had always been a cosy pattern of anticipation and secrets. In the first years of my life, Christmas time crept up on us in the darkness, the half light of cold December unrelieved by any glow of warm light anywhere. As night fell, often before the afternoon was over, the houses in the town were blanked out in black invisibility, the gardens, even the streets, all gone in total dark.

On Christmas Eve I was always put to bed early, and I waited impatiently in the gathering night for the first sounds of Christmas. These were nothing to do with church bells or sleighs and reindeer, but the quiet of the dark suddenly breaking with a hush of muted voices as Aunty Gwen and Doreen turned into the Circle cautiously picking their way through obstacles and puddles. Although I always knew it was them, I still crept to the window to see the tiny bright shadows of two torches, the glass of each taped with white paper and bobbing about along the line of privet hedges like glow-worms on half power.

It was cold standing at the window on freezing lino. As night lowered its chill over my world, the rime of frost would begin to form outside the windowpane. When the two aunties began to fumble with the latch on the front gate, then I would slide back under the covers and gather the warmth of the bed about me.

In this year of the deep snow my excitement had a dull edge to it. I had known for some time that Christmas presents had more to do with the aunties visiting after my bedtime on Christmas Eve than with Father Christmas stomping about on the roof prior to sliding down the chimney. Even Mar had long ceased telling me that she had heard the commotion of a sleigh making a rough landing on her roof and that she'd found reindeer prints in the garden. I fell asleep to the sound of murmuring voices downstairs.

This year, Mam and Dad had decided that I was too sophisticated for the pillowcase on the end of the bed routine, so I woke to find a stack of packages on the chair beside my bed. At least, I thought it was a stack, but it turned out to be just two parcels, each from multiple donors which brought on a tinge of disappointment, but I attacked the wrappings eagerly enough. A piece of cloth, in a rather dull pattern of blue and grey.

'We thought you could make that up yourself in a nice skirt. Or I'll ask aunty Doll,' Mam said practically.

The second parcel was a pack of knitting wool, also a dull blue.

'Jumper to match you can make.' Mam tried to inject some enthusiasm into the occasion.

There were actually several Postal Orders I received as Christmas presents, but Mam just waved them quickly under my nose like a magician on a dodgy trick. She had all these marked down for conversion to National Savings Certificates, because money was for saving, not spending.

So that was the excitement and now it was over. When Mam went back downstairs, I lay back and shed a few silent tears for the things that were missing this year. Where was the mystery of the odd shaped package? Where was the thrill of discovery, of finding a gift that had been patiently stitched or constructed to produce something that was otherwise unobtainable in days of shortages and rationing?

Underlying all these questions was another though; was this what it meant to be grown up? After all, I wasn't a kid anymore; I was at the Grammar School now and Father Christmas was a fairy tale from childhood. Life was becoming more of a practicality than wishes to dream on.

To round off Christmas, the magic world of snow was fast disappearing in the more familiar damp and misty days of winter. Luckily for me I loved reading, and the gloomy days without sun passed quickly as I immersed myself in other worlds of my imagination.

I was curled up on the settee, lost in adventure, as I gently rubbed my itchy feet.

Suddenly Mam pounced.

'Your feet are peeling,' she hissed, rubbing vigorously and removing several sizeable strips of skin. She was right. It wasn't painful, but quite fascinating to discover how long a piece I could peel off.

'Right down the surgery with you.'

I couldn't see what all the fuss was about, but I was bundled up in layers of clothing and hurried over to the bus stop. This was odd too. Normally we walked the two miles to the surgery; it was only for 'rather worrying' symptoms that we took the bus. I kept telling Mam that I wasn't ill and felt OK, but she was deaf.

Dr McKay's examination was brief.

'Oh she's had scarlet fever. But she's over it now. I'll give you a tonic.'

And that was it. I took regular doses of the foul tasting tonic and continued to peel like an over ripe fruit. It reminded me of how I'd felt at Christmas just past. Shedding my skin was quite symbolic; now I really had cast off childhood. I was grown up almost.

I knew instinctively too that this was the last time aunty Gwen and Doreen would come creeping softly to the house with all the stored and hidden presents. In future there would be a more prosaic exchange of gifts rather than the surprise of toys. Father Christmas was firmly relegated to the domain of kids, patiently sending letters up chimneys and believing that every wish was heard, watching and listening for movement in the night sky or the clatter of reindeer hooves on the roof. Even Mar no longer had the privilege of sightings.

The excitement and fever were over. The coming year marked a passage into a different world.

The Time of my Life

'Put your liberty bodice on mind.' Mam almost caught me in the act of stuffing the hated garment under the bed. If ever there was a misnomer, 'liberty bodice' was it. In grace, chic and style it had absolutely nothing to commend it. Like a fleecy flak jacket, the only colour available being that of an old sheep, it was worn over my vest and under my top layer or layers of dress. It (supposedly) kept at bay the howitzers of winter – the chills and coughs and assorted chest ailments which lurked, armed and poised to strike in every bite of winter wind and glint of frost. Secured by a row of closely spaced rubber buttons, it defied any but a concentrated effort of fastening and unfastening and was impossible to wriggle out of. It offered me as much freedom as an ancient embalming bandage.

'Ne'er cast a clout till May is out,' was Mam's reply to any plea for an abandonment of winter swaddling as April budded and began to blossom under warmer skies. I used to try to confuse the issue by indicating the profusion of May blossom well and truly out and about in the hedgerows, but Mam was not one to take chances with ancient saws.

So I was stuck in my button-through duvet until May 31st – unless I could manage to extricate myself and stuff it under the bed before I went to school and remember to produce it with the rest of my clothes when I undressed at night.

Another line of pursuing this argument for emergence from my cocoon was to find out what time it was. If it was past skipping time and coming into hec (hop scotch) time I stood an even chance of gaining my freedom a day or two early.

I ran up to Mar's house to check on the time. For a week or so now it had been kite time, but I sensed the stirrings of change. The enthusiasm was waning. Nothing like the way it had started. Waiting for Dad to come home from work and dragging him out to the back yard with my bits of string and newspaper, watching wide-eyed as the miracle took place. First the two canes, thin and light, cut from one of the large bushes of orange blossom bordering the garden. While Dad tied these together to make the frame, I made a paste with flour and water, then as he used this to glue the newspaper over the frame, I tied small bows of newspaper into the tail.

At last, out on to the green for the test flight. No hanging about, no shuffling apprehensively on the stone curb, right into the middle of the thick tufted grass we went where we could be clearly seen by every kid in the neighbourhood who didn't have a dad smart enough to know how to make a kite. Dad was smart in other ways too – I was the one who had to do all the running about into the wind while he jiggled the string and shouted instructions. Here, I could try to build up to a climax by lying about how we struggled for lift off again and again, but when you live on top of a hill under windy Welsh skies, there was no such contest. Up and up went my kite, with a tease of dipping and bucking wildly, snaking across the gusts of wind, thrashing its tail in delight when I took control. Each pull on the string seemed to draw the rest of the street kids from their houses towards me.

The excitement came not only from making this newly created object dance in the sky as it pulled and tugged so hard to be free, but also from being at the very centre of attention of children who wheedled and pleaded, 'Gis a go then', 'Less 'ave a turn', or more persuasively, 'you can 'ave a go a my 'oop if ew like'. Oh thrill, where have you been in days since then!

But time passed, and suddenly 'kite' days were over. It couldn't be hec time because that came before kite time, so it must be whip-and-top time or skipping time. I had to know for sure so that I didn't go to school next day incorrectly equipped and all behind the times.

'Whip-and-top,' said Mar decisively. 'I went down my cousin's yesterday and we played whip-and-top then.' So it was agreed. Out came the wooden spinning tops and then we had to hunt in the hedges to find good sticks for making whips. Altogether it could often take quite a few days to prepare for whip-and-top time. There was the stick to find and cut and a good strong piece of string was needed to make the whip. So much of the wartime string was thin and wispy stuff which disintegrated after a couple of cracks at the spinning top, so drawers and cupboards were ransacked for a bit of the quality item. Then a nail was needed for the point of spin on the top, and lastly there was a great swapping of coloured chalks for drawing patterns that would whirl and merge and constantly flicker as the top spun. By the time we got all this sorted to our satisfaction, lo and behold, it was skipping time.

At least this was simple. All we needed was a discarded washing line or a reminder of where we'd stored away last year's skipping rope!

Interwoven in all these time slots came tag, hide and seek, and simple Simon. From spring to autumn time raced through the seasons, teasing us and tricking us with days of rain and cold to keep us indoors, unable to enjoy the full allotted sub-season of one or more of our activities. Then the days shortened to wintertime and I was back in my liberty bodice. But at least I knew it would soon be Christmas, and I always knew what time that was and could even count the days.

The mystery was that this sequence of annual activities was never devised or set by any rule; it was born of instinct and tradition and just seemed to happen in the same set order every year.

Sing Before Breakfast, Cry Before Supper

'Stop treading on the cat,' Mam called upstairs to me. We didn't have a cat. Ah, it was Mam's way of not appreciating my singing. 'Sing before breakfast, cry before supper,' she added. I didn't care; in two weeks, one day and three hours I would be setting off for camp, my very first holiday away from home on my own! (Staying with Gran and Grandad overnight didn't count.)

I set out my collection of 'things to take' on my bed and checked them with my list of things to take, and added two safety pins. I had recently started doing this every day, even though Mam cleared it all away in her tidying up after breakfast.

'Can't leave it lying about like that. S'pose somebody come to call and the house not tidy?'

I never understood this logic. Even when anyone did come to call, they never got as far as my bedroom. But Mam was firm in the belief that any visitor, be they neighbour, acquaintance or relation, would know if a corner of the house had been neglected in the housework routine. I am convinced that the ground rules for MI 5 were laid in our neck of the woods.

'Don't think she gives the bedrooms a good do too often.' Sniff. 'Her dusters are out drying on the line before dinner most days.'

'You should have seen the fluff in her rubbish bucket last week. Must have been under the bed for a month.'

Mam dreaded to give the slightest cause that any such comments might be made about her and was meticulous in preventing it.

Going to camp, for me, was a special privilege. I'd joined the Girl Guides as soon as I was ten, the minimum age, but Captain had stated that eleven was the age for going to camp. However, she was in sympathy with my obvious enthusiasm, dampened by this pronouncement, and suggested that I try appealing to our District Commissioner. Appealing to God would have been simpler; all I had to do for Him was to get on my knees, put my hands together, plead a (reasonably) clean record and pray really really hard.

Mrs Powell, the District Commissioner, would require more effort that that, but I knew what I had to do.

Mar expressed great solidarity and loyalty beyond the bounds of friendship.

'I'll come with you if you want,' she said, 'but I'm not saying anything mind.'

There were still some limits.

We set out after one of the weekly Guide meetings. It was evening and early enough in the year to be quite dark, but the brightly lit main road out of town held no fears. It was when we neared the turning to Mrs Powell's house that our resolve took a beating.

Mrs Powell lived in a large detached house in the woods above the church, reached by a broad footpath through the trees. By day it was a delightful meander through leafy beech trees giving kindly shade and shelter from sun and rain alike. The dark and the sudden absence of street lights transformed it. To Mar and me it was an alien land, secret and sly with its whispers and shadows and twisted tree roots eager to trip and fell any who entered this world.

But this was my last and only chance. Grasping Mar's hand and waving my torch with theatrical bravado, I turned my back on the bright street lights and headed for the dim glow of what I hoped was a lighted window of the house.

We stumbled upward in silence till Mar began, 'There's ghosts in these...'

To shut her up I began to sing one of the Guide marching songs. We were nothing like in step, but it had the desired effect until we were through the garden gate and the lighted house stood before us. I had to blink back tears of relief when Mrs Powell invited us into the hall and listened to my request.

'So, you two came up here on your own did you?' I nodded. She asked a few questions about Guides and Mam and Dad and seemed to x-ray me from top to toe with her eyes. Apparently satisfied, she reached a decision.

'Wait here,' she said. She returned very quickly with a form which she said my parents should sign, and opened the door.

'Does this mean I can go to camp?' I dared to ask.

'Remember, this is a Special Privilege,' she replied, 'so you will have to behave specially well. And there'll be no coming home till the end of the full week.'

Downhill is so much quicker, particularly if you run. Mar muttered again about ghosts and took off as if the devil was at her heels, while I floated behind on a cushion of joy with a form to protect me from all ills.

The waiting time was forever, but at last I was able to put my collection of 'things to take' together for the last time and stuff them all into a brand new kit bag – no rubbish this, best army surplus – and I was ready for adventure.

Mam's farewell echoed round my head till I was in the next street and could just hear the sounds from the railway down in the valley.

'Mind the grass isn't wet. Make sure you keep your vest on. Don't get your socks dirty…'

It seems strange that I had never been on the 'up' line of the railway in the Rhymney Valley, only 'down' towards Cardiff. From Pengam High Level where we boarded, the train had one long pull up towards the Brecon Beacons, and all its puffing and straining produced little speed. We passed the pit at Bargoed with its clanging clatter and dust, where lines of coal laden trams crisscrossed each other like busy black beetles. The valley was now a giant inky slash through the piled slatey tips, where rows of dilapidated shabby cottages seemed to sprout from their sides and reach to the valley bottom. It was after Dowlais Top, a great bare expanse of hillside where only the tough tussocky grass flourished beyond the rusty iron railings which enclosed a short wooden platform for passengers – if ever there were any – that the land began to soften.

Soon there were scattered trees beginning to huddle together to form woods, then fields with thick hedgerows and placid cows instead of the tough mountain sheep.

Tal-y-Llyn Halt was the end of our journey. We had been warned there would be a two mile walk to the camp site, but it was level all the way. The sun shone, the air was fresh and so clean to taste, and the fields were laid out with patterns of daisies and buttercups through the lush pastures.

Mam was wrong. I had been singing all day and nothing could spoil the euphoria, and by the time we reached camp there wouldn't even be time for a cry before supper.

The view from the camp site which was already sprouting dozens of tents pitched by earlier arrivals, gave tantalising glimpses of Llangorse Lake in the distance flashing in the sun before the heavy backdrop of the Brecon Beacons.

But all this would have to wait. Upon arrival, I was immediately caught up in the highly technical activity of putting up a bell tent for six of us to cries of 'fasten your line', 'slacken off', and 'fetch another peg!'. It was hard to know who was shouting what at whom and our post-war lack of experience was somewhat obvious. Then of course I had to make up my bed with its ground sheet and sleeping bag – a far cry from wriggling between clean sheets and having someone to tuck the blanket and eiderdown around me. I might have started the day as the youngest camper, but all this put years on me. Regardless of the hard ground, I slept the sleep of the righteous and the dead.

Breakfast was in a huge barn at the back of the neighbouring farm, and we feasted on bread, margarine, jam and freshly boiled farm eggs. Rationing of many foods was still with us, so we were much impressed by such lavishness. Another triumph of delight to begin the day.

The hours were a time of constant discovery in our surroundings and organised activities, all of which sharpened the appetite for suppertime to a degree where it could have sliced bread, but I was in for a shock.

For supper there was macaroni cheese, and I did not, definitely ever eat cheese in any form. The shock was that no one was the least bit bothered or sympathetic. This was suppertime, supper was macaroni cheese and you either ate it or you didn't. There was no Mam to rush for something else from the larder, and the only thing in my throat was a hard lump of tears. I hoped I would fade away to death before breakfast. There were silent tears of misery and self pity in the dark that night, and I certainly cried before supper because I hadn't had any.

Before long sleep came and carried away the memory of such hardship, and in spite of my ravenous hunger for breakfast, the new day promised fresh adventure. Today we would hike to the top of the mountain in whose shelter we camped.

There was one small snag though; when I crawled from my sleeping bag and opened my mouth to speak, there was no sound above a creaky whisper. Unbelievably, and Captain seemed to think carelessly, I had lost my voice overnight. It didn't prevent me from walking though, and as we trudged up the lower sloping meadows of the mountain, I suspected that Captain was beginning to regard it as a bit of a bonus.

The climb soon became more challenging; there were the great clumps of tough mountain grass to skirt, rocky outcrops to scramble over, sudden streams springing from the ground to catch the feet of the unwary. We strove, we conquered; the only thing missing was a row of sherpas strung out behind us towing (oh, dreamy thought) an ice cream van.

We came upon the farm quite suddenly. Breasting another ridge we were abruptly faced with a gate in wall, behind which hens pecked in a farmyard and a black and white sheep dog regarded us with one eye, one ear cocked as he bathed in the sunlight striking the barn entrance. A stone and whitewashed farmhouse stood just beyond, and the dog halfheartedly woofed a warning of our presence to whoever was at home. It was enough to bring the farmer to the door, casual visitors being a rare occurrence this high up and away from the road.

My first sight of him was a picture of flat cap, knobbly stick and gaiters, otherwise he was just like Granddad with his easy unhurried walk, sharp eyes set in a bush of eyebrows and gravely voice. I croaked when he said, 'Hello' to me and this seemed to set his day alight with excitement.

'Just the thing for that,' he said, 'wait here.'

He almost hurried to the house and returned gingerly carrying a jam jar as if it were a Ming vase. The contents appeared thick and unctuous.

He placed the jar reverently in Captain's hands. 'Cured in a day,' he declared with solemn conviction, then tipped his cap and turned to the barn to indicate the interview was ended.

As we returned to camp, Captain prattled on about country wisdom and singled me out before I could make my escape.

'I wonder what the dose is?' she was muttering to herself. 'Oh well, a teaspoon is always safe.'

Willing hands urged me forward, and as I opened my mouth to protest, the spoon found its target.

'Swallow!' ordered Captain. The choice was swallow or choke so I swallowed. Goose grease. It was the most foul tasting, disgusting substance I had ever experienced. I was too paralysed with shock even to throw up, and my eyes watered.

It was as well that Mar was at camp with me. I couldn't cry in front of Mar; it would be up and down the street in no time, and the word 'wimp' would have been invented at least a generation ahead of its time. I concentrated my thoughts on hoping for a supper with a good strong flavour, like onions or mince with a thick gravy and lots of Oxo.

In the event it was neither. It was macaroni cheese. With the taste of hell still in my mouth and throat, this was more dislikeable than revolting, and aided by a hunk of bread dipped in ketchup, I explored the glutinous mess on my plate. Actually, it wasn't that bad if you thought 'ketchup' when you ate it.

When it was time for the usual hot sweet cocoa before bedtime, I drank as many cups as I could lay hands on, not so much to take away the taste of goose grease as the memory of that taste.

Since Captain had promised me more of the same the next morning if the cure was not effected, I vowed to get up early and hide in the barn till she got tired of looking for me.

In the event, I didn't manage to wake up early, but when I did wake, to a bright sunny morning, the power of speech was with me. Again Captain declared herself greatly impressed with the goose grease cure, but I was utterly convinced that a combination of shock, dread and will power had done the trick. This view was further confirmed, if that were possible, when we met up with the hill farmer and his dog in the village. He must have heard me chattering, because he called across the street.

'Rubbed it well in did you? Nothing beats a good rub on the chest with goose grease.'

I could think of a billion things to beat it, and more than a trillion to beat swallowing the stuff.

One look at Captain's look of frozen horror instinctively told me this was not the time to speak. But she did give me an extra toffee from her sweet ration, forgot to tell me off a couple of times and enquired most solicitously after my health at regular intervals.

The rest of the week flew by. The sun shone, we played rounders and team games, rowed on the lake, took turns at cooking and chores, sang around the evening fire and under a canvas roof listened to the night sounds of the hills and fields around us and talked long into the dark. And I ate Welsh rarebit – voluntarily. Quite nice it was with ketchup.

The whole experience was a turning point of sorts; childhood was slipping away. The achievements, the heartaches, new friends, loneliness, were all the sharper because they were mine alone to accept and cope with. No familiar patterns of home to help absorb them and dull or sharpen the feelings. And now it was the last day and we left our adopted home reluctantly. The camp stayed very largely as it was, ready to receive another group of Guides already beginning their various journeys up through the valleys.

From pretty Tal-y-Llyn Halt to bleak Dowlais Top the train chuffed steadily, then ambled down to the lower slopes into the land of coal. Our kit bags weighed heavy as we walked the last mile along Black Path, all upwards, and when I reached home I sat on the front lawn and fell asleep, exhausted but well content.

At the Guide meetings, we lived on our camping experiences for weeks to come and autumn slipped by almost unnoticed.

I was fully engrossed in beginning my new school life at the Grammar School, with all its new rules and responsibilities, and the weeks sped.

It was almost a surprise to be reminded by Captain that Remembrance Sunday would shortly be upon us. I say 'almost a surprise', but no one in the town could stay unaware of the approaching anniversary.

Fighting in the war had only ceased two years before, and as the autumn faded, a current of sombreness seemed to rise and swell in the shorter grey days as the town went on adapting to peacetime. People were quieter in their reflections on daily life, and the youngest were bemused and uneasy with their inability to miss those they could not remember and never could know.

At our next Guide meeting we practised for the parade, and I was overwhelmed to be chosen to carry one of the flags. Thank goodness Mar would be carrying the other.

By the time the day arrived, no one in the town was without a poppy, which seemed to be either a mark of grief or a badge of guilt in surviving. My metal Guide badge and my shoes were polished as never before, and, with Mam checking every detail of my preparation, I left the house far more immaculate than was normal for any ten year old.

I remember nothing of the parade to church; I could only think and see 'flag' – balanced for minimum discomfort on my leather belt. Thank heaven it was a dull colourless November day with no wind or rain, and without incident Mar and I were soon lined up behind the other flag bearers on the church path, ready to make our entrance when the congregation was settled.

At last the organ struck up our tune, soft and solemn for our progression up the aisle to the altar where the vicar stood waiting to receive the flags and place them in silent tribute at the rear wall.

The pressure of the occasion with all its responsibility weighed far heavier than the flag. There was total quiet in the church, not a cough or a rustle anywhere; the aisle was now a mile long, our pace nerve-squeakingly slow and all eyes were upon me.

Suddenly I heard a hiss, a whisper from Mar. I simply could not believe what I heard. How could she? Whispering in class at school was one thing, a bit of a laugh, but this…! The explanation came with a jolt – literally.

Before the choir stalls were two steps and over them an intricately carved wooden chancel, and as each pair of flag bearers reached the steps, they slowly dipped their banners under the arch and advanced to the altar as they raised them again. All except me.

Mar had tried to warn me, but my sense of occasion blocked out everything except following the pair of heels ahead of me at the proper pace and distance. The jar as the metal Guide badge mounted on the tip of the flagpole hit the carved arch went right through my body and stopped me dead.

Desperately I stepped back to right the flag, and the metal badge hooked itself round a piece of delicate tracery becoming firmly wedged. It can only have been divine intervention which narrowly stopped the following boy Scouts from joining the entanglement.

The organ which had been playing soft and solemn music for the slow procession, raised the music a little in tone and volume while first the choirmaster then the verger came to my aid. I don't know which was the worst to bear in my predicament, the swelling music or the total silence of the congregation. Then Mar had a nervous fit of the giggles, and with a panic stricken lunge forward I was suddenly free. The choirmaster and verger staggered, off balance, but my desperate prayer was answered and they did not fall over. At last the flags were in the safe hands of the vicar, who did not betray his feelings by so much as a twitch of muscle, and I was free of that treacherous badge of honour.

When we collected our banners to march to the Cenotaph, mine almost scraped the floor of the church rather than risk a repeat performance.

At the Cenotaph, thanks to all our rehearsals, everything was perfect, the flags in unison slowly lowering for the two minutes silence. Here, however, it was the memory of the town's important folk, the business owners, pit managers, councillors, standing bareheaded in the cold with tears on their pinched closed faces for those they would never see again, that was to stay with me.

The raw emotion and pain was so far beyond my own experience and I never knew that men could cry. Dimly I sensed the touch of grief and wounding that could never be changed, and it softened the abrasive rub of my own heartaches that past summer. My memories and feelings would change. I would grow up. If I cried before supper my tears would be dry by morning, and I could sing again, but these people, for all their success and status, had their tears forever.

Net Chords

The war was over at last. A bewildering time for me and my friends, since in our young lives we'd never experienced peacetime, except from the inside of the pram perhaps. There was no more part-scared, mostly-excited shouting of 'one of ours' every time we saw a plane in the sky, before dropping flat among the buttercups in the field, just in case we were wrong. The shortages, 'making do', blackout and air raid warnings were all part of a huge game really, and in the comings and goings of war the permanent absence of those friends and relatives who had been killed had yet to hit home.

The mine in our Welsh valley hummed and rumbled on as always, but the small American camp which had come to be such a permanent part of our community, had suddenly upped and disappeared almost overnight. Rationing was still with us, but there was such a feeling as of bonds being loosened that we were not quite sure how to cope. Where there had been a rule there was now a gap to fill.

In our restlessness, we dared to venture out of sight when we played together. Was it our infancy or the tensions of wartime that had previously limited our playing area to the back gardens and the field beyond in one direction, or the street with its large green in the other? Perhaps a bit of both. Now we sensed a new and unfamiliar feeling of freedom in the air and we wanted a part of it. We narrowed our choices down to either exploring up the mountain or going over the 'stute.

I had never been able to connect the 'stute (or to give it its proper name, The Miners' Welfare Institute), with the black faced men in dirty clothes who plodded up from the town, puffing and coughing after the climb. Dad was not a miner, so wasn't part of the system of 'subs' from the wages which went to build and maintain these cultural and recreational centres in each community. I have always carried a feeling of great respect for these institutes, and an even greater regret to see them in decline.

The big wrought iron gates at the entrance to our `stute were the tallest I had ever seen in my whole life – not that there were many to be seen in a small Welsh mining town in the 1940s. I had never walked through and beyond the gates. Somehow that was forbidden ground though I'm not sure why. Perhaps the Social Club section inside was a bit too close a connection with pubs and other sinful places, occasionally and obliquely alluded to by Mam, with a sideways look and tight lips.

But all I ever saw of the `stute, as I scuffed past through the overspill of a wide gravel path, was the start of a lovely garden, full of flowers rather than cabbages and swedes.

It never crossed my mind that it was also a place where the Demon Drink could be had – even on Sundays.

My friend, Joan, had a dad who worked down the pit and was a star member of the `stute Bowls Club. It was her idea for us to over to the `stute.

'Sometimes they got pop for 3d a bottle,' she said, dangling the bait. 'And there's a penny back on the bottle,' she added after a suitable dramatic pause.

With such a solid, irrefutable economic argument the choice was made.

Mam always said I wasn't to go out of the street without asking, and she always said 'no' anyway, unless it was to fetch something she wanted from the corner shop. Time had come to step out of childhood onto the path toward teenage rebellion. So I went over the 'stute with Joan – without asking.

We stepped through a small side gate beside the huge wrought iron entrance. I was relieved. I'm not sure I'd have had the courage to push open those huge gates and walk through to where the flower beds began. How could anyone equate that blazing scarlet bed of tulips, shimmering like raspberry jam in the making, with coal miners and their dark pits. I paused for a second to wonder at the sight, then hurried after Joan, who was unlatching a gate in the middle of a white wooden fence buried in pale budding roses and honeysuckle. This was the entrance to a sacred place – the bowling green, a vivid plateau of unbroken sward of green, overseen by a rickety wooden pavilion banked up in one corner. Even Joan would never tread here, but this was not what brought us to the 'stute.

Below this plateau was a large area of broken concrete, enclosed on three sides by a trampled wire fence on high banks. Earth and weeds broke through gaps in the concrete like an overcooked filling beneath a cracked pie crust.

At first, with the bravado of great daring, we enjoyed racing up and down the green banks that were rich with dog daisies and buttercups, the long grasses snapping against our legs. Mam came and fetched me three times, nagged a bit, then gave up. Since the 'stute was halfway to Jones the Grocer anyway, we could compromise by me doing a bit of fetching of essential supplies. This in turn taught me a valuable lesson in the hiring of labour, for chasing up and down the banks was thirsty work. With the temptation of cheap pop on offer, I now had expenses as well as adventure, so Mam and I reached a wage agreement.

From the start, Joan and I always went together to get a bottle of pop. It needed courage to walk along the terrace in front of the main building and approach the front entrance. This comprised two wide stone steps scrubbed porridge white and double wooden doors with brass fittings as big as pump handles.

Trying not to leave finger marks on the gleaming brass, we crept into a cool and silent hall. On one side was a beautifully carved mahogany staircase, overhung by a central chandelier catching slivers of sunlight to scatter about the dim interior. There was no carpet, just richly polished floorboards challenging our dusty shoes. It was even more imposing than the Headmaster's room at our local council school, a room I'd only just glimpsed when my particulars were taken for the Scholarship Exam.

From the hall, holding our nerve, we entered the Den of Sin – the billiard hall. We sidled, giggling for courage, around the doorpost within easy reach of an open hatch. Resolutely keeping our backs to the darkened room, where shadows moved beyond a white glare from which an occasional muted cheer of triumph or muttered oath of defeat drifted through the tobacco smoke, we exchanged our pennies for pop and scuttled out. We would worry about the ordeal of returning the bottles and claiming our deposit later. Pity that for us curfew time clicked in before the chip shop opened.

Soon, we were well into Spring and the evenings were growing longer. We were becoming bored with running up and down the banks and looked for more sophisticated pleasures.

We started by throwing an old tennis ball at the racks and fissures in the concrete. We could never have offered a 'shilling on the side' to make it more interesting, but we did invent a system of point scoring for every crack hit fair and square.

Then somehow we each acquired an old tennis racquet. Joan's was a bit twisted and had very few strings, mine had slightly more strings and the novelty of an old fashioned fish tail handle. It had once belonged to Aunty Doreen, and Dad had rescued it for me from Grandad's shed. Mam was pleased too. So far we had used our hands for bats when playing, and apart from the burden of extra scrubbing of hands being lifted from Mam, she thought it much more ladylike to use the racquet.

'There, you can play bat and ball proper now. In college Aunty Doreen had that!'

Doreen was the brains in the family, the only one ever to proceed past primary education, to secondary, then college to become a teacher.

Mam left her very roughly basic village school at twelve, and to see me with Aunty Doreen's tennis racquet made her feel as proud as if the Queen had called to borrow her teapot.

Contrary to the rules of any recognised court game, we aimed to keep a rally going between us for as long as possible – not an easy objective with our equipment! It was considered a bit off to hit the ball beyond the other's reach, and to make a fair game we swapped racquets from time to time.

Peggy and Caleb from the next street had now joined us, so two would sit on opposite banks holding up a line of string across the 'court' which made it easier to judge who had failed to keep the ball in play. It was all a great help in taking our minds off the biggest ordeal in our lives. Soon we would sit the Scholarship Exam.

Apart from the tuppenny fare bus journey, one mile up or down the hillside between our street and the town high street, I had never been on a bus on my own. Come the day of the Exam, I had the Big Adventure before the Great Ordeal; there was a four and a half mile bus journey to the Grammar School where the Exam was to be sat, then almost a mile walk, most of it well nigh vertically upward.

The night before I checked and re-checked and checked again that I had everything as per instructions, fountain pen (an encouragement birthday present), fully filled but with a bottle of ink (in case), pencil, rubber and ruler. These were packed in a small attaché case, borrowed as in the fashion of the rest of my contemporaries from a relative, and necessary more than anything for the wadge of sandwiches done up in greaseproof paper. As long as the exam didn't run more than a week over its allotted day, I wouldn't starve on my sojourn beyond the street and the valley.

Dad went through the bus times with me like a repeat of my times tables, and Mam made absolutely sure that I had clean underwear ready and dazzling white socks. I was more prepared than a rocket on a space launch.

As the bus filled up with children clutching their Exam equipment, street and valley solidarity bound us together in groups ranging from feigned nonchalance to trepidation and quaking terror. I remember nothing of the journey, the exam papers, or the Grammar School, except for one vivid picture; there was a huge rectangular lawn, more than twice the size of the 'stute bowling green and equally lush, smooth and level. This led on to three tennis courts, side by side with proper straight lines marked out in heavy white, each court with a taut central net and not a hole to be seen.

This was posh, this was real tennis – my ambition to pass the Exam and gain entry to this world was hot.

We returned home, our street gang of five, faithfully returning each sandwich, a nibble or two removed from the centre where it hadn't completely dried out. We hadn't dared throw them away. We had been born into an era of rationing which was only just beginning to end and to waste food was a greater sin than anything which would bring a policeman to the door. Or even the vicar or chapel minister.

Another summer was in full blaze, flowers ousting the glut of turnips and cabbages from the gardens, bringing colour to the streets after the dark years.

We children were bigger and taller now, and over at the 'stute we held the string higher and higher and the balls flew across harder and with straighter aim. With the end fence flattened by age and rust, we often spent more time searching in the long grass of the field beyond for lost balls.

Looking back, I'm surprised that not one of us found fame as a civil servant or a politician since we seemed to spend more time making up the rules than actually playing a game.

One day, Mr Williams descended upon us while we were playing. Great apprehension. Mr Williams ruled over the whole domain of the 'stute outside the billiard hall and those big double doors. He made the roses bloom, kept hedges in line with military discipline, and as the seasons changed, he had some mysterious power to cause new swathes of colour and shape in the flower beds to appear as one faded. He also tended the bowling green, that sacred carpet of green velvet where devotions took place on Saturday afternoons, and sometimes during the week when the evenings were light enough, as long as conditions of grass and weather were approved by Mr Williams.

Just the sight of that bowling green improved our accuracy of shot with the tennis ball tremendously.

Any wild hitting in that direction meant that the ball often ended up on the green, and there was an inflexible rule binding us that 'he (or she) who hits it, fetches it.' It proved impossible to fetch that ball without feeling the lash of Mr Williams' tongue. Even though we crept towards the green with shoes off, no matter where he was – at the back of the pavilion, kneeling in a flower bed with his back turned, behind the roses – he always knew when a ball landed on his precious turf. From where we stood, you didn't tangle with Mr Williams for a number of reasons. First, and most important, he possessed power of entry. On Saturday afternoons, when bowling matches took place, he couldn't banish us far enough. It was alright if he was playing in the match, then we would gradually sidle along to the pavilion and ingratiate ourselves with the tea ladies by fetching buckets of water for washing the lettuces and filling the tea urn. This rewarded us with a quick knock up on 'our court' while the bowling teams sat about with their cucumber and lettuce sandwiches and cups of tea.

Over that first summer, we won over the confidence of the tea ladies sufficiently to be allowed to grope through endless quantities of lettuce leaves floating in bowls of water, searching for grubs and other potential uncooked meat sandwich fillings, and to wash up. Eventually this patronage gave us enough protection to stick around even when Mr Williams wasn't playing.

The other weapon Mr Williams possessed was his power of invective. When he just wasn't in the mood to have his peaceful afternoons among the flowers disturbed by a bunch of noisy brats squealing and jumping about, he could chase us off, arms flailing, waving a frayed straw hat, with a flow of language describing our uncertain pedigree and very certain destiny should we not take flight instantly, without ever repeating himself.

Thirdly, Mr Williams was in charge of tickets. This meant that no one could use the bowling green or even our broken up old court without first digging Mr Williams out of the appropriate bit of garden in order to get a ticket to play.

When he issued tickets, Mr Williams would go into the 'office', a cubby hole at the end of the pavilion. He would then begin his ritual. First, the bottom section of the door had to be shut and bolted so that he could rest the roll of pink paper tickets on it to do business. The cash went into a tobacco tin, secured with an elastic band, and retrieved from among a collection of flower pots, twine, other tins in varying degrees of rust and odd clips of crumpled yellowing paper, the whole lot netted together with cocoons of old cobwebs and dead flies. Oh, such power!

On good days he'd let us play on the court for free, but on not so good days he charged each of us 1d, but without any time constraint. On bad days, like after a bowls match that had roughed up his beloved green, it was 1d each per hour. If we became too absorbed in our game to be aware of the time, life could be very expensive.

Finally, there was Mr Williams' place in the social hierarchy, of which we were just becoming aware. We never discussed it, but we each, at that time, had an instinctive feeling for our place in the community. I think it must have been a kind of 'head and hands' method of gauging where we fitted into the social order.

At the lower end were people who worked with hands and feet; they walked to work and laboured manually all day long. Then the order rose to the level of the people who rode to work in varying degrees of splendour, be it bus, bike, car, pony and trap, or horse, and were judged to spend their days thinking about what the rest of us should be doing. Everyone else had their slot somewhere between the two.

My father, like those of most of my friends, was a 'hands and feet' man, and Mam was in some awe of anyone who wore a collar and tie to work and/or used transport to get there. Consequently, Mam believed irrefutably anything told her by the rent man, the insurance man and the vicar, but tended to argue with the baker's boy and the coalman, and was quite uppity with Tommy the Wash, who was not a laundry man, but came round regularly with an old push cart to collect potato peelings and any other suitable kitchen waste to feed his pigs. (Not that there was much waste in those days!)

Mr Williams was a puzzle because he didn't fit into the system as we saw it. He worked with hands and feet alright, but the power of the man was out of all proportion to such a lowly position. Why, even the captain of the bowls team wouldn't give the go ahead for a Saturday match without Mr Williams' say so!

As he stood on the bank watching us, we felt uncomfortable under his gaze. We became polite and unnatural with each other. Caleb bit back his retort to Joan's accusation that her shot would have gone over the string if he hadn't suddenly twitched it higher.

My return shot was nervous and the ball hit the edge of a large crack and shot up over the bank onto the bowling green, rolling to the middle and lying there as out of place as a pickled onion on a wedding cake. Not a chance of denial or foisting the blame elsewhere. All eyes, including Mr Williams, were on me. That 'Great God of the Bowling Green' lifted his straw hat to scratch the back of his head and jerked his thumb towards the pavilion. My so called friends were clearly of a mind that I was on my own as I forced my shaky legs to climb the bank and follow the back of the straw hat that was now rapidly turning into the black cap of the hanging judge. The best I could hope for was quick execution rather than be subject to any one of the unmentionable fates wished upon us, from time to time, when Mr Williams was in one of his black and loquacious moods.

I would not, indeed could not, cross the pavilion threshold, not the way I was quaking. I watched as Mr Williams rummaged under the whole conglomeration of string and flower pots. What was he looking for? Whip? Branding iron? Boiling oil?

With a grunt of success, he backed out with his arms full of string netting. My legs buckled as he dumped the pile on me and sent me packing with just one growled admonishment to 'Keep that bloody ball off the green' . The relief gave me enough courage to rescue our ball before returning with my treasure.

We now had our ball back plus a real tennis net! OK so we had to extend the ends a bit with string and fix it to a couple of tent pegs hammered into the banks, and it was a bit ragged and it had a pronounced droop in the middle, but no one could deny that it was a proper tennis net!

We immediately adjusted the scoring system so that hitting the net lost a point, but hitting the ball clearly through a hole in the net without touching any part won a bonus point. Our game had now reached new heights of refinement. To hit a bald tennis ball with a saggy stringed racquet through a hole in a droopy net, causing the ball to bounce at a winning angle from a crack in the concrete, let alone reach the climax of 'game set and match,' the only technical language we knew when it came to scoring, required considerable skill and concentration (plus a touch of luck). Really, Wimbledon is too easy!

Towards a Goal

The summer evenings flew by as we honed our skill at our game of tennis, pushing memories of the Scholarship Exam further and further back into the dark days of winter.

Then one day at school, the Headmaster strode into our classroom in the middle of a lesson. We dutifully rose in a ragged wave of apprehensive movement. Unless you were in the top class, apart from morning prayers, the Headmaster was only ever seen at close quarters by those waiting for the cane or those who, on request, came with orders from their mams for the rhubarb, apples and other various seasonal fruits and vegetables that the Head produced in surplus from his garden. For him to interrupt a lesson it had to be serious – or a glut of lettuce.

There were many sidelong glances directed at and from suspected miscreants, but we were all wrong. The Head was there on a matter of much greater gravity than truancy, fighting or greengrocery. He had in his hand the results of the Scholarship Exam.

But first we had to suffer one of the Headmaster's lectures on Effort and Attainment, normally delivered with monotonous regularity at morning prayers when the full set of around one hundred of us squashed into a space euphemistically described as a hall. He droned on about Effort and Standards and Hard Work, but like the rest of the glassy eyed class, my mind drifted off.

I had given little thought to the future in the golden days of that summer. The present was all that mattered, with each moment to be seized and filled. The rhythm and co-ordination I was aware of in my body as I aimed my rickety racquet at the ball, the excitement and thrill of satisfaction as the ball sped away, was total delight. Our little gang, almost double in membership now we had a net, was happy and harmonious. No matter that our equipment severely limited speed and accuracy; after all we had nothing to compare with, for television had not yet invaded our homes and Wimbledon was merely the name of some place in England where a lot of other people played tennis. We had our own World Championships at least three times a week, and twice on Saturdays if bowling permitted, when we were all together. Caleb said that he, Peggy, Joan and myself were the seeded players, being founder members, but I failed to see what we had to do with gardening.

And now suddenly, like slamming shut a book in the middle of a long story, the Head stood before us waving a piece of paper like Chamberlain coming from Munich.

But this was no peace promise, this was the pass list of the Scholarship Exam, the key of the door to the post-war world. To fail meant a move to the back water of the 'top' class, simply marking time with filling inkwells and stacking milk crates in the corridor until a birthday was passed and a niche was found in the outside world. The pit for a boy, a shop counter for a girl seemed to be the ultimate career expectations for those who were not destined for the rarefied atmosphere of one of the Grammar Schools. Oh, I passionately did not want to go on to filling inkwells till I was ready to stand behind the drapery counter of Mr Jones the High Street.

The wide-eyed fears and dreads, well stirred by playground chatter, of being faced with impossible subjects like foreign languages and mathematics, ropes to climb that went – oh, a hundred feet high, and homework; all these were gone in an instant. Please let me pass, oh how I wish I'd worked harder.

The Headmaster was reading the list of names, and I wanted to be sick. Then he read out my name and I nearly was. The Pass List, and my name was on it. My mind stopped its crazy whirling and focussed on one thrilling idea. Now I would actually be taught to play real tennis on a proper court and, oh yes, my destiny no longer led to the drapery counter.

The whole family seemed turned on its head. Mam and Dad had little experience of education, each entering the adult working world at the age of twelve. Dad looked pleased but said nothing, just worked longer hours for extra money to fulfil a long list of equipment and school uniform.

Mam, whose own opinions could often be turned at a stroke by the opinions of her 'betters', wavered between quoting the insurance man and Councillor Griffiths. So one minute it was a 'waste of time educating a girl, they only go and get married and someone else reaps the benefit', the next it was 'we're putting something valuable in your hands that nobody can take away'. It was as if I was about to start filling an intellectual bottom drawer with Mam's prize cut glass vase from the front room mantelpiece stuffed up my jumper.

Gran was the most bewildered. She and Grancha (who never offered any opinion) had come from traditional occupations of miners and housemaids, and she was convinced that no good would come of this leap to middle class values.

'Just remember,' she warned Mam, 'she's a working man's daughter and always will be.'

To add to her bewilderment, of her seven grandchildren, the three boys had failed the Scholarship, while the four girls had passed.

Every Sunday we used to walk up the hill to Gran's house. It was two miles, all uphill and she lived in a rented farmhouse just below the old church and cemetery. To judge from the size of the church, St. Sannan's, with its old Norman tower, there probably once existed a fair sized community, but now it was a scattered hill top hamlet where the three local pubs were in a ratio of about one to every three houses. It did have a dog track though which probably saved the pubs from extinction.

Families visited the cemetery on Sunday afternoons, and with the advent of peacetime, a bus service was introduced, up from the town at 2 pm and 4 pm, back at 3 pm and 5 pm.

We rarely caught the bus. Mam regarded it as an indulgent extravagance to save walking a mere two miles. On the few occasions we did ride, it was because it was raining particularly hard, and I was being sulkily rebellious, yet again, about these ritual visits.

I was beyond the age of being 'seen and not heard' and when the weather was wet there was no chance of playing out in the fields. We all sat in the big farm kitchen where the social intercourse was always the same; uncle Bill spitting in the fire at regular intervals interspersed with Mam sighing that it 'looked like raining for the week' and aunty Lil making grave economic forecasts on the price of bread, meat, fish and other exciting commodities. I would be given three old copies of the 'Red Letter' bodice ripper magazine and be expected to sit, head bowed and silent for the duration of the visit. Gran just sat and thought a lot and threw in the odd suggestion of what might be available for tea.

Tea was the high spot of the afternoon. Because of rationing, everyone contributed something to the table. It was all very discreet of course. When we arrived, Mam would disappear into the larder with perhaps the back end of a tin of fruit sticking out from under her cardigan or clutching a rustling paper bag, then aunty Lil and whoever else came to call would go through the same surreptitious motions.

The spread that came out of the larder was always lavish. The centrepiece was always a huge plate of Welsh Cakes which all the aunties praised as being superior since they were baked on a proper bakestone over the fire. I couldn't taste any difference but I was smart enough not to say so.

There was a big garden around the farmhouse where Granddad spent most of his time aided by uncle Bill, and as the seasons came we had fruit tarts of rhubarb, apples and damsons, crisp pickled onions with home-cured and cooked slices of bacon, and deliciously flavoured scrap-fed, scratch-in-the-field roasted chicken. Best of all were the bowls of strawberries, fresh picked with the warmth of the sun still on them, the flavour far superior to those which have had all the taste chilled out of them now that we are so obsessed with refrigeration.

It was on these occasions that the signs of the coming break with family tradition began to show. Mam always listened to her Mam, whose word was law. If Gran showed disapproval of a new hat or dress, it would never be worn (at least not for best) again. Judgements on actions or circumstances were declared 'right' or 'wrong' as decreed by Gran's code, the way it always had been in the family tradition.

Now suddenly Gran was faced with four granddaughters being offered the chance to pursue courses of knowledge and learning leading to undreamt of careers, independence even. Such a waste, and such a poor preparation for marriage.

'No good will come of it. Educating a girl above her station is a useless sacrifice.'

By all the rules the very idea of this educational leap should have died right there, but for once Mam defied her Mam's pronounced advice.

The same was true for my cousins, and, in fact, Denise, aunty Lil's daughter, won a State Scholarship to Cambridge later on. Perhaps it was just as well that Gran wasn't around when that happened.

For Dad, I think, there was never any question to consider; I was simply following in the footsteps of Aunty Doreen, his sister. She was the only person so far, in either family, to have gone to college. Indeed, her teaching career afterwards was so successful that she would one day be awarded the OBE.

I never heard any discussions about my future at this stage, and having passed the exam, it never occurred to me that I would not take up my place at the Grammar School.

Agewise, I was just approaching the level of education that Mam and Dad had reached. At the age of twelve, being able to read, write and add up with reasonable competence, Dad had joined Grandad in the building trade to learn carpentry, and at the same age Mam went to help on a milk round until a position was found for her in a local drapery shop.

Mam couldn't understand why I had to have half the stuff on my school uniform and equipment list – or any of it for that matter. Special gym shoes and navy knickers for games and PE indeed. Did they think we were made of money?

The general uniform was alright. That was 'smart' and would mark me out as Grammar School material, altogether brighter than your average candle, and a cut above most of the street.

Everyone went to Hunts the Saddlers for their school satchel. This was made of tough strong leather, and one Saturday afternoon I was taken to choose what Mam had decided I was having.

I liked Mr Hunt's shop. We always went there for my summer sandals, brown leather with crêpe soles and a side buckle. Not the best in comfort, but at least they were lighter than my winter lace-ups. Intermingled with the overpowering smell of leather, were the whiffs of rubber and resin, drifting from the oilskins, horse tackle, sportswear and boots for sale.

Once the business of choosing the leather for my satchel was over, we had to get down to the more interesting negotiations of buying gym shoes.

Mam extolled the merits of the thin soled flat black ones, daps as they were generally known, while I went straight for the high tech white ones with cushion soles. To hell with gym and PE! I could only see the white canvas footwear flashing about the tennis court, whereas Mam could only see the price tickets, 5/= as opposed to 10/6d.

Mrs Evans from our street came unwittingly to my rescue. She had come into the shop to buy some shoe laces and Mam didn't want her thinking we were cheap.

'Mind you keep them clean,' she admonished me as she passed the white shoes over the counter for wrapping, plus of course a block of 'Blanco' for whitening the canvas tops.

Mrs Evans said nothing so she must have been impressed.

All the time we were in the shop I didn't dare browse openly amongst the section where the tennis racquets were kept; that would have been asking too much. The price tags started at 30/=, but one day, oh yes, I'd be back.

By the end of the summer holidays I was ready. The gym shoes, by this time, were well worn and thoroughly whitened. Just breaking them in.

My blazer and gymslip had been bought 'on the big side' to allow for growth, so the sleeves on the blazer were turned in a couple of inches and tacked down, and the double hem on my gymslip felt like a spare tyre.

The blouses were a nightmare. Aunty Gwen had always had an eye for a bargain, and the magic words 'Ex-service, Surplus' acted like iron filings to a magnet. I'd had a dress and petticoat made from parachutes, and a 'new' navy top coat with the bottom cut off drastically and the sleeves re-designed to fit in this way. The trouble was that Mam and Aunty Gwen were so obsessed with length, they never thought about width, and the coat appeared to be as broad as it was long. I was never so glad to grow out of anything. And oh, those blouses! They were ex-Wren issue, 'lovely quality, washes a treat', with detachable collars. I was instructed to tuck the trailing shirt tails into my knickers, while a generous tuck was put into each sleeve to allow me use of my hands.

By a superb piece of inspirational psychology and manipulation of the facts, I convinced Mam that they were just not in the style of school blouses, and incorrect uniform was a hanging offence. I also think that the sight of me, bulging knicker-tucked and half-handed, was too much even for Mam. I pointed out that the official school blouses could be ordered at Jones & Richards, the town's main store, so Aunty Doll made my blouses. They actually fitted me, for which I was eternally grateful. Right from the start, in spite of Mam's hopeful optimism about allowing for growth, I knew there as no chance of me growing enough, and in the right directions too, to take up the slack in a knickerful of shirt tails and four inch tucks in the sleeves – especially as I only had a month before starting my new school.

Fortunately, there was no such thing as an ex-service gymslip, this being obtainable only at Jones & Richards. That gymslip and the blouses were the first clothes I can remember having brand new and in a size that fitted (with just a tiny minimum of tucks for growth), what with the intrusion of the Second World War into my life with its restrictions, shortages, rationing and the endless 'make do and mend'. Anything that wasn't handed down or altered by Aunty Gwen came in a parcel from Canada to our next door neighbour, or a parcel from America to aunty Lil. Luckily, I was smaller and younger than the kids next door and my two cousins. Some garments, often quite strange and of dubious use, were made from nylon parachutes. If only this had been the age of punk fashion. I'd have been a wow, but I was years ahead of the fashion.

Now that I was properly kitted out and equipped, I could concentrate on my new world.

The Grammar School had begun as an endowment from the wealthy and powerful Lewis family of Glamorgan in the 1800s. Its aim then was to educate, that is teach to read and write, a small number of boys from poor families in the Pengam area. This was so successful that it was decided to include girls, but heaven forbid that the two sexes should mix in the same building! So, safe around the shoulder of the mountain and higher up, my school at Hengoed was created for the benefit of the female sex. Those early days set high standards, in which failure was never considered or tolerated, and as the school expanded, it took pupils from a wide area up and down the valleys, opening up entry into professions never dreamt of before.

After being given something called a timetable indicating set times, places and subjects, I couldn't wait for the first games lesson. I might get lost and late scurrying about a layered maze of corridors, seeking out classrooms, but an expanse of four tennis courts could hardly be missed. These were a smooth un-pitted vista of tarmac, each court with a taut unbroken net, all the same height, all the way across. But there was a shock in store for me.

At the appointed time for games, we were all assembled at the edge of the courts – then marched out of the side gate next to them and up the mountain road. It was a long, steep walk, our aching legs chivvied and harried by a teacher who did not suffer weaklings or whingers gladly.

The road led us to a field straddling the hilltop. It was muddy, bumpy, thistley, windswept from every direction and had sheep scattered about. I was handed a bent stick with a net on the end. After the punishing vertical yomp up the mountain, now they wanted me to play lacrosse!

I did not enjoy the experience. Still wallowing in disappointment, I was given a set of games togs. This ensemble consisted of a putty coloured vest, a kind of fore-runner of the T shirt, and dark brown, heavy cotton directoire knickers. It is possible, with the boys' school only a mountain top and a mile away, that these passion-killer garments were designed to deter any hanky panky, but since we didn't play rugby with the boys and they didn't play lacrosse with us, this theory is not too tight.

Either way, the outfit was not very conducive to chasing about our mountain top playing field waving a lacrosse stick. If the elastic in the knicker legs was tight enough to keep them tucked up under one's bum, it tended to cut off the circulation of blood to the legs; if it was slack or loosened with wear, the legs slid down, over one's kneecaps, impeding progress. My elastic was of the slack variety and no amount of rolling and hitching up would allow me a decent turn of speed up the pitch to the distant goal mouth. Strange as it may seem, we were playing the game because a previous Headmistress had decided that it was a more ladylike game than hockey. I sometimes remembered that when I got a whack round the head or the legs with stick or ball.

I tried very hard to learn to play lacrosse, because I quickly cottoned on that one was either a sports person or a swot. The swot image displayed a general lack of enthusiasm for physical activity, being awkward and clumsy in the gym, and swots were constantly nagged to greater effort by the PE teacher. What was more to the point, they had no clout when there was a choice of PE or games or when the insufficient equipment was shared out. Swots seemed to spend their games sessions doing a forced run up to the games field and back. We keener types (well, me anyway), could by a show of willing eagerness ingratiate ourselves to a point of taking part in what we wanted to do.

I had calculated that if I huffed and puffed up and down that tussocky lacrosse pitch and grunted enthusiastically on the netball court all through the winter, I would one day be able to get my hands on a tennis racquet, preferably one of the new ones I'd glimpsed in the games cupboard, not yet even unwrapped, rather than a warped one with strings missing. I really felt that my competence with a racquet deserved that.

At the end of each term, the last day's morning Assembly was extended for the ceremony of Posture and Appearance awards. There was no Gold Cup, but each recipient was given a small stripe of navy blue and silver, about three inches long, to sew on to the gymslip. This was supposedly a recognition of our efforts at Pride in Appearance (i.e. school uniform), and Not Lolling About in Class, but we all knew that the balance of choice lay in the Games and PE department. It was a much coveted award, particularly in the lower school; anyone who had not gained a P and A by the time they reached the third year had to be a complete wimp (or rather, a swot, to use the language of the day).

On the first occasion at the end of term, I was full of a mixture of hopeful excitement and fearful dread. Like everyone else, I longed to be chosen, but if I was, it meant having to go up to the platform to receive it.

Being in the first term of the first year was bad enough. You were at the bottom of the heap, the lowest of the low, and the best method of survival was to creep through it and avoid drawing any attention to oneself.

Receiving a P and A broke all the rules of first year behaviour. It was physically stepping out of line in the well ordered ranks of school Assembly and mounting the platform to be the object of all eyes.

The platform was a raised dais at one end of the school hall. It was just big enough to support a lectern with its large leather-bound Bible and a polished oak table behind which the Headmistress sat on an impressively carved oak chair. At the back were deep blue velvet curtains through which the Head made an entrance each morning, black gown flowing about her like smoke following a genie as he popped from a bottle. Her sudden appearance always had the effect of cutting all murmurs and whispers like double glazing on a draught.

To make matters worse for anyone 'called to the platform', there were two sets of removable oak steps, well worn and well polished, one set for up and one for down. For the most part, being presented with a prize or award was the nearest a pupil ever got to the Head, and as no one was ever allowed (or ever dared try) to mount the platform except on these rare occasions, it was pretty nerve wracking at any stage of school life. Already, in my own short time at the Grammar School, I had felt keenly for those 'called to receive', as they tripped or stumbled on the polished steps and boards, or in their nervousness used the wrong steps for going up or down. It hardly lessened my awe when I discovered much later than the Head did not actually swoop down from some lofty pinnacle to make an entrance through the curtains; she merely came through a door at the back of the staff toilets.

I stood very still throughout the hymn and homily, dreading and hoping. I listened to a general chiding about walking on the forbidden lawn, wasting school milk, and not removing hats on the way to and from school. Then I listened to an account of achievements for the term, and at last, at long last, the Head picked up a list of names placed beside a box of blue and silver stripes. My name was not on the list. My acute disappointment was slightly mollified with relief, but I was determined that my time would come to mount the platform. So I didn't get a P and A this time. So what. I had just watched a lanky fifth former receive a very impressive enamel badge as School Captain of Netball. One day, I decided, I would be going up those steps as School Captain of Tennis. And I did.

Getting Ahead

When I arrived at school in the morning, I entered the playground with some trepidation. Children had already started gathering in small knots of gossip, huddling against the cold.

I hoped that Lydia wouldn't be around, at least not until I'd met up with my friends, but my luck was out.

A stick like figure, clattering along in over-sized boys boots that had no laces, suddenly shuffled out from behind the air raid shelter and barred my way. Aggressive, unpredictable, unwashed, underfed and dressed not so much in hand-me-downs as tossed-aways, Lydia was a character we all feared.

Hindsight is a wonderful gift and it's easy now to realise that Lydia was a product of harsh poverty, born to wartime when even in the most desperate of times the country could find no use for either of her parents, illiterate and ignorant beyond finding their own salvation. The local pub seemed to be the only beneficiary of their existence.

Surprisingly, perhaps, truancy was not a problem in Lydia's family, with the five children, three brothers and two sisters of junior (or 'big school') age, attending regularly. Possibly the chief reason for this was the free school dinner they all enjoyed, which I daresay was their only meal of the day, for they all had that thinness and grey pallor of the undernourished.

But Lydia was tough. Any slight, real or imagined, to herself or her family, and Lydia retaliated with fists and feet unfettered by scruples. If a day went by with no insults, she would join in any old fight to put some fire into it.

My aim, as always, was to get to school either with a couple of friends, or slide in alone and reach safety in their numbers.

'Wanna fist in your chops, girlo?' was Lydia's friendly greeting. I shook my head to decline the offer. Fortunately this time Lydia quickly lost interest, and having stuck out her tongue, went back behind the air raid shelter out of the wind. Breathe again.

I was lucky that day perhaps because Lydia had hair. Events followed a regular pattern. The 'nit nurse' visited school and inspected all heads. Of those in my class, Lydia was one who was not seen for a day or two after the visit, then re-appeared with a woolly pixie hat covering her shaven head.

Mam brushed my hair and had a quick inspection every morning, and occasionally made an unpleasant discovery. When this happened I knew that when I came home from school, a tearful encounter with a nasty bottle from the chemist's awaited me.

But I never dragged my feet, nor did I struggle and whine; all I needed was to hold fast to the image in my mind of Lydia in her woolly pixie hat, friend of no-one and whispered about by all. I've never like hats.

Mam, on the other hand, loved hats. Before she was married, she sold hats in The Bargoed Emporium, the most prestigious shop in the neighbouring mining town, with a branch in Blackwood.

Hats were status; they were proper, nice, smart, posh, ladylike. So I suffered.

The winter was OK, I had a variety of pixie hoods, some all of one colour, but most made from oddments from unravelled garments, every one an individual design of flamboyant initiative. They'd probably fetch a fortune today as designer knitwear. Anyway, it was cold in winter, and the hilltop where we lived was exposed to the wind from any direction, so I didn't mind being tied into my pixie hood, often with a scarf over the top, just to make sure my ears didn't freeze off.

Summer Sundays were the real bugbears when it came to hats. First it was off to church. I vividly remember the straw 'poke' bonnets with ribbons that tied under the chin. They were always hot, uncomfortable and had sharp bits that scratched. If it happened to be Whit Sunday, we all had to parade through the town to church, after Mam had dressed me up in a new dress and bonnet with extra sprigs of artificial flowers all over it.

When we came back from church for Sunday dinner, I still wasn't finished, because in the afternoon we always walked 'up top' to Gran's, me in my Whitsun best, and I had to look nice and walk tidy till we got there.

On Sundays, Dad left his working cap on the peg behind the door under the stairs. He put on his best suit, grumbled about the starch in his shirt collar, and spent a long time in front of the mirror on the hallstand, knotting the tie Mam had told him to wear. After combing his hair and making a straight parting, he plastered it in place with brilliantine and sat in the best armchair with his trilby hat on his lap, waiting for Mam to get dressed.

Sunday was the only day of the week Dad was able to sit in that chair without Mam darting ahead of him with 'a bit of cloth to save the cushions!'. I was never quite sure what she was saving them for or from, but perish the thought of Dad's working clothes coming into contact with those cushions! I asked her about it once, but she answered with a question which implied that the answer was patently obvious.

'And what if we had a visitor?' she said. You'd think that all this was quite unnecessary since they'd been through the process once of changing clothes for going to church in their Sunday best, but with Sunday dinner to serve and an hour's work in the garden before it was ready, working clothes were back in mode.

Mam always took ages to get ready. I wasn't allowed to play outside in case I got dirty, so I sat waiting, kicking the legs of my chair, which would earn me a telling off for scuffing my shoes. At last Mam came downstairs.

'What do you think Perce?' she asked, turning her head this way and that to display her hat from every angle. Dad grunted something like, 'It'll do nice.'

'Oh, you're no good to ask,' she said crossly and disappeared upstairs again. This was repeated two or three times until they were barely on speaking terms, then Mam rammed the first hat back on and attacked her hair with a comb until it obediently clasped the hat in a tight roll, like a bent torpedo. A couple of hatpins secured the whole arrangement as tight as if superglued, and then we could go.

In winter, it was a long walk up the mountain road to Gran's, but this was summer and dry weather, so we could take the path across the fields, cutting a few corners.

First, we skirted the edge of the American Air Force camp along the far side of the Showfield. I was not to understand why this field was so called until after the war when funfairs and agricultural shows picked up their annual habits again.

I liked walking to Gran's this way. We took the footpath across the golf course into the old lane, then through a farmyard and several fields until we crossed the main road to the large grazing pasture where Gran's house stood.

As the summer progressed, there were always flowers to gather. After primroses, violets and bluebells, came dog roses, honeysuckle and the delight of finding patches of wild raspberries, wimberries and strawberries, followed by great thorny swathes of blackberries. And all the time there were stiles and kissing gates to negotiate, banks of sheep-cropped grass to slide down and cowpats to dodge.

Within the iron clad discipline of corset and Sunday clothes, Mam soon began to wilt and had to hang on to Dad's arm. By the time she'd been lifted over the second stile, she was giggling.

Everything was fine till we reached the main road, then Mam called me back.

'Don't tell Gran I've got a new hat,' she warned grimly.

'Why?' I asked.

'Because,' she replied closing the discussion. I knew I wouldn't understand anyway. There was grown up logic involved in many explanations like this, and it was beyond my years.

When Aunty Lil had called a few days previously, the same hat had been flaunted, admired and bragged about far beyond its worth and beauty. Now it was different.

'This old thing? Course you've seen it, our Mam.'

I left them to it and went to play in the hay barn. I'd heard it all before, with coat, shoes, dress or anything new.

To Mam the hat was everything. As long as she could have a new hat,

I think she would have gone to church naked – well in her old working dress maybe.

This attitude contrasted with that of Aunties Gwen and Doreen, who never ever discarded a hat. They had a huge cupboard, gloriously full of hats, which gave me hours of preening and dreaming. I was also fascinated to see them re-modelling hats, cannibalising them, disguising age and shabbiness with ribbon and flower sprays, or – disappointingly – just dusting off the mothballs and wearing them again after a long enough period of cupboard purdah.

The Scholarship Exam results came that summer. I wanted to pass because I didn't want to be left behind when all my friends moved on, as I was sure they would. Cefn Fforest Council School had a good records of results, but to fail meant a drift into the Top class – a misnomer if ever there was one. Top class was an assortment of individuals who had nowhere else to go, having had their chance to progress and missed their one bite at life's cherry. They would be eager only for the day when they could either go down the pit to become a man, or get a job in a shop and wait to become a wife, according to gender.

The Scholarship said 'those who knew' would give me freedom beyond imagination to make choices in my life.

The relief of passing the exam led on to a summer's preparation of kitting up for the new school. With all the aunts drawn into the pool to stitch and knit as much as possible, not a week went by when I wasn't being measured, fitted or studied for a growth allowance estimation. There were things to buy too, one store for this, another for that, the most impressive being an order with Huns the Saddlers for my leather school satchel. Not just any old one of many satchels, but one with my initials tooled into the flap. How personal could you get?

After many dress rehearsals, I was ready for the first day at Grammar School. Mam checked me out like a security guard on a bonus promise, then I was let loose in plenty of time to catch the bus. Mam made me check one more time on the doorstep – new bus season ticket, leather satchel with my initials prominently but casually on display, top to toe uniform – all bearable, even exciting, except for one item, the navy blue beret. It was tight and itchy.

As part of the school uniform, I quickly discovered it was a capital offence to remove the beret at any point between home and school. Something to do with school pride and smartness we were always being told. I have a theory though that the Headmistress was probably an ex-Commando. She was certainly tough enough. The game of removing the beret, dodgily running the risk of being caught, was a training in itself.

There were times, though, when I thought of Lydia with her often bald head and woolly hat and wondered at the differences between us. What price freedom?

Lighter But Tighter

I was up at Kaff's house, helping her to pick raspberries in the garden. It was a good year for the fruit, which seemed specially sweet and juicy. I was quick on the uptake and eager to help anyone gather in the delicious berries, a task which needed much quality testing.

We were hurrying to finish picking against the fading light, when Kaff's big sister Dorfy came bounding down the path (I really thought her name, as intoned by Kaff, was Dorfy, though in fact it was Dorothy. Something, I think, to do with having a Welsh mam and a cockney dad).

'There's ice cream in town,' she burst out, 'and Conti's is open.'

The news did not have the shattering effect she had hoped for. There had been three popular Italian cafés out of five in town, all shut during the war years, but even if they had been open, our families were not sufficiently economically blessed to wean us into café society. Ice cream we'd read about; it sounded quite nice, but we didn't miss it because we'd never tasted it. Rationing and shortages had precluded the production of such luxuries.

Dorfy was older and more gastronomically experienced than Kaff or I. Her exciting news raised a disappointing reaction from us, which amounted to a laconic, 'yeah?' and a couple of distracted glances. We only thought about it again when we sat in the dusk licking our fingers and eating up any fruit that we judged squashed or nearly damaged. It seemed that wafers, whatever they were, could be had for 3d or 6d and on finding that we could rustle up 3d beteen us, and the next day being Saturday, we'd go down town and gamble the lot on Conti's ice cream.

It was not a winning decision. I found the stuff watery, lumpy, and, in sharing this oblong block of it stuck between two soggy, thin biscuits, half of it ran melting and sticky down our arms or dripped onto the pavement. Give me raspberries any day, I thought.

But in spite of my disappointment with the ice cream, these were heady times; the lights were coming on all over town, not the soft shadowy gas lamps of pre-war times, but bright, sharp as day electric ones. All five cafés were open now, some as late as eight o'clock, and the chip shops offered fresh cod on the menu!

Unfortunately it all affected my economic situation; I had outgrown my royal status – never needing any money because everything was put before me, even a fairly regular supply of sweets. I had negotiated for pocket money, but soon realised that I had underestimated my costs badly. Fortunately, perhaps, sweets were still rationed, which helped to rein in temptation, but Mr Williams was a bit keener these days on collecting the 6d per hour to use the stute's tennis court, and on summer evenings a 6d bag of hot fresh chips between two or four of us when darkness fell was a fitting end to the evening's play. And on wet Saturdays, I could barely scrape together enough to go to the pictures.

Mam was a very tough negotiator. She would not be outmanoeuvred, bullied or bribed. No rise. Now things were going to get tighter still.

We'd noticed for some time that members of the `stute committee seemed to enjoy watching our version of tennis, and on Saturday afternoons when a bowls match was on, we were quite a counter-attraction to the small bands of team followers. The reason for the committee's interest soon became clear.

On one side of 'our' court the bank was much higher and steeper than the bowling green side and led to a large expanse of pot holes and lusty weeds that had once existed as two further tennis courts. The deterioration had set in before the war began, and the state of them now defeated even our inventiveness and imagination.

Then one day, as we played yet another Wimbledon Championship on our cracked concrete with its holey net across the middle, the machines arrived.

As the days and weeks went on, they cleared, dug, levelled and tarmaced the whole surface of the old courts and the white paint appeared. Two courts were carefully measured and marked out and two brand new taut nets completed them as ready for play.

Paradise? Oh yes, but the fee to enter paradise was doubled overnight. One shilling per hour per court ate into my resources. The chips would have to go for a start.

Suddenly, tennis became an adult pastime and there were proposals to form a club. To be fair, Joan, Caleb, Peggy and myself were included in this from the start, as founder members and initiators so to speak, and Joan and I stayed as committee members till we went off to college.

It seemed outrageous that we four had to wait our turn for a court as well as pay double now that a steady stream of adults turned up to play most evenings.

However, there was a financial advantage very often to making up a foursome with often generous interlopers, and it turned out that they knew the proper rules and how to score, so we endeavoured to both join them and beat them.

When the club was up and running, we had a Grand Opening one Saturday, which included a free tea for members and the presence of the wife of the local council chairman. I was chosen to make a little speech and present her with a bouquet. If God had come that day, he'd have been second in the queue – any queue.

It all made life very complicated. I played regularly in the Grammar School tennis team now and I'd had the thrill of being chosen when I was in the second year, an achievement previously reserved for fifth formers.

Logistics, as a subject, did not appear in the school curriculum; I doubt it had even been invented. But I was an expert when it came to Saturday matches, whether school or club, home or away, to dovetail together. It helped that school matches were always in the mornings and club always in the afternoons.

So it went. Race down town for an early bus. If it was a home match, one journey to Maes-y-cwmmer, then race down the hillside to the river and up the 1 in 4 hill, half a mile of it, to school. An away match, perhaps with its crisscrossings of the valleys, usually involved a change of buses or a bus to the railways station at Pontllanfraith. Though often right on time, this first part was relatively uncomplicated. It was the return which was difficult.

I could never be sure at what time the school match would end, and it was important that it fitted with bus/train times so I could be at the club venue for 2.30 pm.

'What about your dinner then?' was always Mam's first reply when I outlined my Saturday activities. I always explained that the schools fed us; I didn't add the details that it was a couple of Welsh Cakes and weak orange squash.

Economic pressure was ever squeezing tighter, though grandparents were often good for the odd extra shilling. Mam was keen for me to put these bonuses in my piggy bank, but they usually went straight to the West Mon Bus Company.

But life wasn't all tennis. The coming of the new bright lights to town brought people out in the evenings. The pubs spilled customers on to the street and there was even a café society sipping their brew as they waited for the start of the 'big' picture (the main feature) in one or other of the two cinemas.

This opened the way for more frivolity, a lightening of life. The Operatic Society, Male Voice Choir, and two drama societies breathed signs of life and we even had our own Christmas pantomime. Now people flocked to the Square Café to experience the new phenomenon of Canadian square dancing in the room above the main café.

Joan and I investigated this once, but all we got was a glimpse of a packed mass of people hopping, skipping and twirling to the commands of a caller! We were barred for being too young. However, I did glean a valuable piece of information. They needed a 'washer upper' in the refreshment area, 8.30 pm. to 10.30 pm.

At first, Mam and Dad would have none of it when I was promised the job if I had their permission. Then Dad went to see the café owners whose house was very near Grandad's. The upshot was that they would see me home, to the first light on our street anyway, and I could start next week.

It was quite a comedown from being (sometimes) the star of one or two tennis matches each Saturday to dogsbody with a wet dish cloth in the café, but at least I was earning money, 5/= as I remember, that would service miles and miles of bus journeys with enough left over for a bag of chips.

Later, as the square dancing craze really blossomed, I was able to change my shift to a Friday night, which left me free to go with Joan, dancing at the `stute. This was the big `stute in town with its own public library, theatre and proper ballroom dancing floor.

Ah, the quick step, foxtrot and waltz – so much more sophisticated than square dancing. We were taught all the steps at school, which whetted our appetites, and we craved the glamour of swinging round the floor in twirling skirts and high heels, so much more romantic than the P.E. lesson where girl clutched awkwardly at girl, each in their plimsolls, brown gym knickers with droopy legs, and fawn vests.

Mam's apprehension and bewilderment increased by the week.

'Pass the Scholarship for them to learn you dancing? Going out Saturday night at a time you ought to be coming in? Down the `stute? That's right next door to the pub!'

As usual, negotiations were long and protracted, ranging through the vaguest allusions to drunken debauchery by progression of many ills to white slavery. Mam only gave ground when her research into the situation revealed that quite a few 'nice' girls went dancing at the 'stute.

'In this house by nine o'clock, not a minute after.' Mam practically slammed the words down with a shovel, but I was prepared for this. After acquiescing meekly, I did casually point out that if I stayed on to 9.30, I could catch the last bus, 9.40, up from town which saved me the dark walk and dangers from admirers and kidnappers alike. An unbeatable argument, and anyway, I knew that with a following wind I could nip up the hill from town in ten minutes and needn't leave the 'stute till 9.50.

Other exciting avenues were extending from the valley all the time. I don't know whether this was initiated by a burst of post-war reaction to the years of dark, closeness and restrictions, or by the fact that I was growing up with a greater awareness of the world. Both probably.

Someone told me about the big east Wales tennis tournament at Pontypool, and, in a moment of supreme optimism, I entered. I progressed weekly through the various rounds taking place at a variety of courts up and down the Valleys, until, unbelievably, I was due to play in the final.

Through sport, we'd formed a small gang of friends, Joan and myself and five of the boys from the boys Grammar School who were occasional tennis partners. They were also pleased and relieved to find Joan and I to be sympathetic teachers when it came to learning to dance. Being dedicated rugby players, they sometimes rushed us down the dance floor like a run at the forward line. One of them, Trev, had passed his driving test and announced that, courtesy of his dad's permission to borrow the car, I would have my own supporters' club at Pontypool.

'Tell you what,' said Vincent, all fair hair and angel face, who often astonished his opponents when he flattened them in a rugby tackle, 'if there's a cup and you win it, we'll fill it for you – cider mind, not champagne.'

Come the day, I was sick with fright. Not only that, but on turning up at the swanky sports pavilion at Pontypool, I was mortified to find that every player, apart from myself, had one of the now fashionable sports bags containing their playing kit. I had merely done what I always did for matches; I put on my pristine crisp and white blouse and shorts at home, then the newly whitened shoes with matching socks, tucked my racquet under my arm and trotted down to town to catch my first bus.

I was the outsider anyway, in this eager group of trophy hunters, but it only helped to get my dander up a bit. I'd fought hard and won my place to play a match for the singles title, and I wasn't going to give that up easily just because my opponent had an expensive sports bag and two racquets!

I'm told there was quite a crowd, but I don't remember. All I do recall is the euphoria of winning a match less hard than I'd imagined, then floating up to a dais to receive a huge silver cup. My band of supporters, faithful throughout with their clapping and cheering, were close by and, as I took the trophy, a stage whisper caught my ear.

'Bloody hell, have you seen the size of it? It'll hold a bucket of cider that one.'

It certainly was the biggest cup I had ever seen, bigger even than the bowling cup in the 'stute!

Later, as we all squashed into Trev's car, I touched my lips to the cup's contents. It was by no means full, but symbolically overflowing with the pleasure of my friends' joy in my win.

They delivered me home to the door and we all tumbled in bearing the prize. Dad took the cup and examined it carefully before pushing Mam's cut glass fruit bowl out of the way to put it in pride of place on the sideboard. He was grinning like the proverbial Cheshire cat.

'Thought she would,' he said to nobody in particular. I didn't think anything could crown the day, but to see Mam fluttering round the room completely speechless as we all bubbled and babbled about, was worth something.

That cup must have cost Mam a fortune in silver polish for the year I held it. Mam had it gleaming fit to put the hallstand mirror to shame, and woe betide anyone who left a finger mark on it!

One way and another, that was quite a year.

Dreaming On

I was too old now for any daydreaming in the daisies on the green; too old as well to steer the old concrete slabs, almost buried in grass through mountainous submarine infested seas, or twist and dive in the sky through squadrons of enemy fighter planes.

Our championship cracked concrete tennis court expanded our world and going to the Grammar School took us further still.

Friendships changed too; Kaff had not passed the Scholarship Exam and was less comfortable with the rest of us as we exchanged tales of new experiences.

Our little tennis gang splintered somewhat, we were divided between three Grammar Schools in the area. Only Joan and I were selected for Lewis School, Hengoed, so this had drawn us closer, especially when the tennis club was formed and we both played in matches.

It was a dark November evening and we were struggling against vicious clouts of rain sweeping down from the Beacons as we walked up from town. We had just enjoyed a couple of hours of escapism with a Hollywood musical at the cinema. It was the clothes that had entranced us as much as the action.

With the coming of peacetime, clothing coupons had been abandoned, and fashion burst onto the scene. No more parachute dresses and cut down coats for me, no matter what Mam said!

'I liked her in that pink swirly one best,' said Joan. I considered this carefully.

'Mind that skirt she had on when they were dancing on the roof was nice. Showed the seams of her nylons lovely. Bare shoulders too! And did you see those heels on her shoes?' I reckoned my favourite was at least as good as Joan's.

We each relived the film's fantasy for a while as we battled the weather, following the action through wind that had never disturbed a hair on the head and rain that left faces dry but for an attractive mist around the eyes. Of course, we arrived home like drowned rats, but who cared?

Since passing that vital exam, we had been coached on a diet of dreams, urged to be ambitious, encouraged to reach for our own star whatever it might be. The war's end brought hopes and determinations for a new equal world and we were urged to gaze upon the kaleidoscope of opportunity on offer to us.

As a girl, I was no longer to be groomed for work in a shop or factory, each occupation with its own aspirations of an early, successful (i.e. prosperous) marriage. Then the word 'career' was mentioned frequently. I could be, say, a teacher if I wanted, or even a doctor, and one day women might even want to be engineers or pilots. Heady stuff.

The first thing I learned at my new school was that dreams begin on the solid ground, not in the head. Just to get there, I took a four mile bus journey, always with a heavy satchel full of books and homework. The bus didn't go all the way either; it stopped along the hillside road at Maes-y-cwmmer to disgorge its school load collected up like flotsam from villages and hamlets along the valley road. We then had a mile to walk, a quarter of it down to the river and three quarters up again to where the school perched on top of the hill.

The three Rs were taken as dealt with; now I had to struggle with a great span of subjects like algebra, foreign languages and sciences. And in all this bewildering introduction, I had to keep my new uniform clean and neat and remember to wear my school beret at all times between home and school. To travel bare headed was an indictable offence. The school rules were tighter than Mam's, with no room for negotiation.

The prosaic and familiar subjects were a welcome relief, none more so than the needlework lessons, as sewing was now called. I was on edge. What would we make? Full skirts? Party dresses?

At first the cookery apron was a great anticlimax. I'd done 'apron' already and was eager for more intricate and glamorous items, but at least I'd learned how to operate a modern sewing machine and the basics of pattern construction.

Joan was in my class and experienced the same frustration, and it was she who came up with an idea to advance our skills.

Her cousin was four years older than Joan and had just made a skirt under Joan's intense scrutiny. After longer discussion, with the added ingredient of our love of tennis, we concluded that we were quite capable of making tennis skirts.

We wouldn't even be using a pattern for such a simple garment, which would cut the cost considerably, and since this could be defined as clothing, we were each fairly confident of a subsidy to the expense involved.

And so it came to pass. I had to measure and cut out under Mam's critical and worried gaze though.

'Special clothes for playing a game indeed. There's old frocks upstairs from last year. You could let them out a bit.'

I was glad to do the sewing on Aunty Gwen's old treadle machine. It seemed to break down a lot, but Aunty Gwen had endless patience and advice for sorting out problems.

At last, with Joan, I could plan my court appearance. No debutante could have been prouder. We were blind to the ever-so-slightly uneven hems and wobbly stitching. No Wimbledon match had a grander start than when we two swept on to the institute courts in our look-alike white skirts.

We progressed rapidly with our sewing, and Mam was quite encouraging. She felt she was saving money on my clothes with the added satisfaction that while I was sewing, it 'kept me out of mischief.'

When we were old enough to enjoy the Saturday night 'hops' at the main town 'stute, we were forever worrying at the problem of what to wear within the bounds of our tight budget. One solution was to make two skirts, one each, from a single length of material in such a way that they looked quite different. Not easy, especially when the luxury of buying a paper pattern to cut from did not make the project economically viable. But it was the spur to our initiative and inventiveness. Designer clothes? We had them all the time at about 3/6d a yard!

Rags to Raffia and Readymade

Mam held up her petticoat from the ironing board and sighed.

'Good quality cotton that was.'

She studied the worn bit which also had a long split down the middle.

'No good for patching or mending, that. Now, rug or duster?'

I understood what she meant The absolute end for any garment too worn to mend was the duster bag, but clothes that had a life of some gentility went into the rug bag.

Rugs were important. We had our 'good' prestige rug made largely from bits of good worsted cloth and heavy cotton, just inside the front door, which conveyed instantly to any caller that no riff raff lived in this house. Then there were the more practical rugs, strategically placed to save the 'good' carpet in heavy duty areas. Carpets wore out far too quickly in these straitened times, and within the parameters of household economies, shortages and rationing, they were not easy to replace. So lo and behold, enter the rag rug, costing nothing except time and patience.

First, we needed a piece of clean sacking, (quite easily come by), a hooked tool and all the garments that were beyond being shortened, lengthened, patched, darned or cannibalised to make another. These were then cut into strips and knotted into the sacking to form a plump and multicoloured rug. It was a slow and laborious job, but as was the custom, the whole family took part.

Aunty Gwen, the patient one, would spend hours at it, and seemed to turn out rugs at factory pace, and Mam often made the excuse for not visiting neighbours that she planned to spend the evening on the rug with Dad.

I liked rag rugs. They were thick and soft to sprawl on with no sharp reminders from Mam that my wriggling or spilling of a drink would wear it out and there would be no replacement 'for the duration'. That is, except for the one which took pride of place before the hearth, and had nothing but the best rags knotted into it, from Mam's old best frock to Granddad's best quality pre-war flannel shirt. As I contemplated glimpses of my own and other people's past times, I was constantly urged not to spill, drop or shuffle on it.

'Lovely quality, my old second best frock in that.' Mam would reminisce.

But at least I didn't have to wear a rag rug. My worst experience of 'new' clothes was having Aunty Gwen and Doreen's garments cut down, taken up or otherwise altered so that they would somehow hang together on me.

Thank heaven wartime rationing precluded many parties with the attendant worries of 'what to wear'!

The alternative to being kitted out by the aunts was having clothes made for me by Mrs Thomas the Sewing. This was not only cheaper than 'ready made', it saved on precious clothing coupons.

Then the war years gave way to peacetime and began to loosen their parsimonious grip on the market place. Where before, supply of anything was only measured against need, now we could indulge ourselves a little. Rations increased quite generously and fashion in clothes was reborn.

Joan and I were becoming quite proud of our efforts at fashion design and sewing, but accessories were more of a problem. Though we could turn a couple of yards of material into skirts, blouses or dresses, there was no way we could find a piece of cheap leather and turn it into shoes! It's one time I was grateful to be allowed to rake through the aunty's cupboards and come up with a pair of court shoes that were no longer wanted. They didn't fit too well, but the suffering was worth the feeling of grace and glamour.

In spite of Mam's reassurances on how smart they looked, I just refused to go to Sunday School parties or square dancing in my high fashion homemade dress with flat school sandals and school satchel as accessories.

However, privation and desire are good spurs to initiative, and it wasn't long before we found the answer (or part of it) in milk bottle tops.

I don't remember where the idea came from, but soon we were hoarding these tops by the dozen. There were several sources of supply. Milk always came in bottles, delivered to every house, though only two per day to our house. The mother lode for yielding milk bottle tops was at school.

At that time, even when war ended, every school child, come morning break, had a bottle of milk containing one third of a pint. Some loathed the milk, some loved it, but there was always a rush to the crates. Each bottle was sealed at the neck with a cardboard disc which had a small inner 'push in' disc. The resulting hole accommodated a drinking straw and the outer ring was left intact in the bottle. These discs were prized and pounced upon.

We all grabbed for and hoarded our treasure till we had enough. It was slow going, and each top had to be cleaned and dried, but when my tally reached fifty I judged myself to be ready. Now I could buy the raffia!

Each disc had to be completely covered in raffia, knotted round like a knobbly tyred cartwheel, then they were stitched together in rows, folded, shaped and stitched again to form a bag.

'Lovely shopping bag, that,' said Mam.

'Handbag,' I replied.

We compromised. Mam could see that there were nothing like enough tops for a shopping bag, but made me promise to make one for my second creation.

Those raffia covered milk bottle tops seemed to spread through the valley from end to end, like a virus. They fell out of books, satchels and school desks, littered every surface from school playing field to the nooks and crannies of every home.

They were even left on buses. But slowly, the results began to show.

My newly fashioned bag had lively sophistication and flair I was sure, and swung nonchalantly over my arm every time I sashayed like a Hollywood queen into town. It seems odd though that with the quirkiness of human nature, although in my life pre-raffia handbag my pockets were always stuffed with bits, pieces and 'things,' I found I had nothing to put in my bag. Make-up did not feature yet in my life, I never had any money, so what else was there? Perhaps just one item. Girls grew up accustomed to keeping a clean handkerchief tucked up a knicker leg, until maturity produced a feeling of gaucheness in raising one's skirt, however modestly, to grope round the side of a buttock prior to using the said handkerchief. I knew that handbag would be useful for something!

So much in life goes in circles, and new accessories led back round to the main wardrobe. Sometimes alone, sometimes with Joan, I cut and stitched to the pattern of images in my mind with varying degrees of success.

With all this discovery of fashion, tennis, school and my expanding social life and friendships, life raced on towards college. Being a year older than I, Joan went off ahead of me with Mar, but time for me raced even faster.

I was soon looking to buy second hand books, equipment, clothes and a huge wooden trunk to put everything in. This stood in the front room as Exhibit A, inspected willy nilly by every visitor to the house. Just in case anyone thought we were fooling, Exhibit B was my letter from the London (yes, London – planets away from Blackwood) College accepting me for the three year Home Economics course, qualifying me to teach.

With a little persuasion, Mam had to agree that I needed a good 'best frock.' I was smart enough never to use the words 'evening dress,' but I knew what I was aiming for.

Perhaps Mam realised that I had outgrown Mrs Thomas the Sewing now with my grown up shape having more complicated curves. She made her decision.

'We'll go to Cardiff and look for a nice frock, ready made.'

So the time came, a month before I left the world of the Valleys, and we went shopping in Cardiff, I thinking 'dresses,' Mam thinking plenty of underwear for keeping clean and a sensible warm nightie.

I hung on to my patience as we went from one store to another, feeling, pulling and comparing the prices of underwear till Mam was satisfied and decisions and purchases were made.

Then the 'frock' department in the best store in town. While Mam fingered a modest garment in a light wool with a neat collar, I was drawn to what I could see as the only dress in the store. It was created from layers and layers of chiffon and tulle, shaded in all the red and golden hues of flickering flames, nipped in to the waist then rising to a strapless bodice. Even Mam was struck dumb. I think for a moment she was eighteen again herself. I touched the material and the dress whispered to me of glamour and romance far beyond my experience.

'Go on then, you can just try it on if you like.'

I stepped into the dress and my dreams and twirled before the mirror. The fit was perfect and I was all my Hollywood heroines in one creation. Mam was very quiet, never said a word in fact; I think she was stuck in her dream too. Casually she glanced at the price ticket and suddenly we were both back in the real world.

'Twenty-five pounds!' Mam could barely whisper in shock.

There was nothing more to say. I, the dreamer knew I could never even contemplate the dress being mine, and changed quickly to attend to more practical things. But instinct told me that if Mam, the sensible hard economist, had had £25 in her bag she would have bought that dress on the spot.

Strange, but now many years late, that creation of fire and light will always be the most beautiful dress I never had, and I still can't remember the good 'best frock' we bought instead.

Parties and Partings

Parties were mixed blessings. On the one hand, they carried the excitement of anticipation of 'the day,' especially a birthday with its gifts and cards. But planning a party needed skill, ingenuity and saving by denial and downright cunning.

There had to be cake of course – birthday or Christmas which would require a whole precious egg, then at least two other kinds of cake. Even sandwiches weren't easy; it wasn't so much the fillings as the scraping on of the margarine eked out of the weekly grocery order. Would there be a tin of fruit? I was always confident of this because Mam kept a small hoard under my bed, but for some of my friends it was quite a worry.

Rationing eased only slowly when peace came, but as each restriction began to loosen, we pushed harder to break it. I think Mam found the Saturday afternoon shopping quite exhilarating at this time; instead of a faint hope that there might be something in the way of a little extra, she trotted down to town in great expectation that there certainly would be – and heaven help Mr Pegler the grocer if he tried to deny her. Perhaps a tin of meat as well as tinned fruit? An extra packet of tea maybe? Mam would expect to have at least half of her wishes fulfilled in discreet 'under the counter' deals. No doubt, as I did, she recalled incidents during the tightest times of the war, like the time Mrs Sharp rushed in from next door interrupting Mam's exertions with a scrubbing brush on the kitchen step, puffing with excitement.

'There's fresh fish in town! Our Cecil saw the lorry going up the warehouse behind the Emporium!'

With that she was off, curlers snatched from hair, empty shopping bag flapping like a sail in a loose wind. Mam wasn't far behind. Fresh fish?

This was a bit of mystery to me and a distant nostalgia to Mam.

Sacking apron on the grass, coat flung over pinny, a hasty turban over brown paper curlers and a sharp order to me to 'Look quiet and sit tidy', and Mam was off at a trot with an empty shopping frail clutched across her chest. It was the first time I had seen Mam leave the house without stockings.

The campaign was a triumph. A small piece of cod was very carefully divided up and reverentially fried with a great pile of chips. Dad methodically worked his way through without comment as he always did, while Mam replayed the drama of Buying a Piece of Fresh Fish, (cod too, mind you) in abbreviated comments between mouthfuls. I enjoyed the chips. The fish was okay, but I wondered if any of the beans would be ready for picking in the garden.

It had been a long haul, but now joy was breaking out all over. Less coupons, fewer shortages, rations comparatively generous – just the problem of finding the money to pay for it all. Words like 'no allocation' and 'off for the duration' might have lost their usage, but habits die hard. For so long any extras in supply had been carefully hoarded, and Mam for one couldn't stop. Every week she bought extra tea and sugar which went into the sideboard cupboard, and a tin of fruit which went under the bed in my room. It was useless to reason why with her; the answer was always the same. 'You never know,' was said with the same nuances of apprehension and uncertainty.

My own affluence was increasing too. Apart from washing up after the dances, I had graduated to a little table waiting on busy nights and then got a job working in one of the chemist shops on Saturday mornings.

This job certainly rounded off my education. There was no training, just straight into a fresh white coat and behind the counter to serve.

Of course, it would just happen that one of my first customers was a man who marched into the shop, slapped half a crown in my hand, then stared at the perfume shelf and waited. Not a word spoken. I tried asking, as politely as I had been told, what he wanted, but he merely transferred his gaze to the toilet soaps and went on waiting.

One of the other more experienced assistants came out of the dispensary at that point and recognised a familiar situation. She politely elbowed me aside, muttering 'wait out the back,' opened the bottom drawer under the counter and took out a small package. Squinting through a crack in the door, I saw the man snatch it with relief and gratitude and leave. In the next few minutes I had an education in what a condom was and how to recognise each of the four regular customers who came in early on a Friday morning and waited at the 'special' bottom drawer end of the counter with half a crown at the ready.

Men of regular habit, all of them, but surely they might at least have said, 'Good morning' without embarrassment. My only worry was that, with my inexperience, someone might just hand me half a crown one day and I'd get confused or over eager when all they wanted was something for a headache.

Peroxide was easier. At that time, a dilute solution of peroxide was used for bleaching hair, and we sold two strengths, 20 volume and 10 volume. I had to get used to one regular lady who always came in and loudly demanded 20 voltage peroxide. At first I was doubly confused, as her hair was dark going grey, and I never did find out what she did with the peroxide. I didn't know what she plugged into her mains electricity either.

It seemed that the white coats we assistants were all required to wear immediately imbued us with medical wisdom, from witches brew to up-to-the-minute biochemistry. Faith in the product was strengthened either because it was very old or because it had a long and unpronounceable name. People didn't just want to buy cough mixtures, pills and salves; they wished to be sold a cure with a convincing argument for its efficacy.

In reply to my confession of ignorance of these matters, Mr Thomas who owned the shop told me to spend time between customers reading the labels on the boxes and bottles. He was familiar with them all, often producing a potion from deep nether regions of the back store room, covered in ancient dust, when with great panache he would reverently wipe away the cobwebs and present the bottle like a rare and vintage wine.

Sometimes a customer, a little embarrassed and flustered, sought a private word in the dispensary with Mr Thomas. Although this door was always open, Mr Thomas was adept at positioning himself and the customer so that not a word was overhead, even by anyone diligently dusting the shelf just outside in the shop area. Why people didn't just go to the doctor with their problems was a psychological step beyond me.

At least my wage negotiations were fairly successful. These took place, not with Mr Thomas, who told me how much he would pay me and I said, 'Right, thank you very much,' but with Mam. It wasn't easy. Mam lived by the tradition that a working man put his unopened pay packet on the kitchen table on a Friday night, and his wife calculated what might be spare after weekly expenses, and handed that back – if any. My problem was that Mam was boss, chief shop steward and household economist all combined, which didn't give me much of a role. Her only weakness was that, since I started working in the chemists, Mam kept producing shopping lists of cures for all sorts of newly discovered ills, all of which had to be paid for. Eventually we settled for a set percentage to be handed over for my keep.

When my birthday came round, I secretly treated myself to a bottle of perfume (10% discount to staff) called Evening in Paris. The shop didn't keep a large stock of perfume, just various Coty perfumes, Californian Poppy and Evening in Paris. The Californian Poppy could make your eyes water at twenty paces, but Evening in Paris even sounded subtle. The male sex would be swooning at my feet, though perhaps with the exception of Derek, Trev and Tom – the rugby prop forwards and half back! It might soften them up a bit though.

So I began to organise my party, which followed the usual set formula. It would take place in that inner sanctum, the Front Room, which of course restricted numbers, ten being a real crowd. This worked pretty well for me. Our gang had settled into a regular crowd which included five boys from the Grammar School at Pengam, and we girls evened up the numbers.

It seems strange today to recall how exciting these parties could be, just talking, necking and batting jokes about that were a little more risqué than usual. Alcohol never featured nor did we feel deprived; we sustained ourselves on a variety of soft drinks and a batch of sausage rolls leading up to the pièce de résistance – a birthday cake, thick with fruit, marzipan and icing and candles to blow out.

As the evening mellowed, our thoughts drifted to the future. Our college and university applications had just been cast upon the waters of hope, and we sat as a gathering of engineers, doctors, dentists and teachers to be. It was an evening that served to remind us how little time we had left in our own small self contained world. The party was over, but life was about to begin, if we just had the wit and intelligence to grab it.

In the event, we all gained places at the colleges of our choice, and it seemed that no sooner had I got over the thrill of doing an adult responsible job for a proper wage, than I was counting the days to the end of it.

Trev was my boyfriend at that time. He would be going to university in Newcastle in September, while I was off to London. It never seemed to occur to us how far apart these places were as summer days sped by with tennis matches, weekly dances at the 'stute or just meeting up with the gang of an evening and putting the world to rights over a bag of chips.

The West Wales Tournament was at Langland Bay, just outside Swansea that year. This was a stroke of luck; Aunty Girlie and Uncle Sid lived in Swansea, and having no children of their own, were always delighted to see me. So, with bed and board secure, I was able to enter the tournament and even pay the entry fee out of my saved wages. For once there was no argument from Mam, for the Sketty area of Swansea where I would be staying was very respectable you know.

Just to add a little icing to the cake, Trev's parents invited me to join the family on their week's holiday in Cornwall, just before Trev and I left for our colleges.

Langland Bay was quite intimidating. First, I discovered there was no bus running early enough to get me to the courts in time each morning, so I had to walk. It was only a couple of miles over the headland, and I quite enjoyed the experience in a week of softly sunny mornings promising bright high summer days.

I'd learnt by now to carry my kit in a sports bag, but I still only had one tennis racquet, while each of my opponents carried at least two.

The chat in the changing rooms was of boarding schools, tennis coaches and following a summer circuit of tournaments, so I had little to contribute, but it all helped to keep my concentration focussed on the game ahead.

Communication was much swifter and more efficient in those days. Mam had an arrangement to walk down to the telephone box on the corner of the Showfield at a set time each evening, ready to receive a telephone call from Aunty Girlie re-assuring her that I had not run off with the milkman, been sold into white slavery or joined a big time crime gang. Oh yes, and I'd got through another round in the tournament that day. By the time Mam got back home, the whole town had been updated on my progress.

My boyfriend, Trev, had recently passed his driving test, and come Finals day of the tournament, he loaded his father's car with the rest of the gang and they all headed for Swansea.

What a boost for me! As a complete stranger to this event, I'd had no faithful band of followers to cheer me through each round, but now I had my friends' highly vocal enthusiasm. Canny as they were, they remembered the lesson of Pontypool, and quickly assessed the size of the cup before they even tracked me down.

'We won't be filling it for you mind, but if you win we'll have a bottle of cider and a fish and chip supper before we drive home.'

You couldn't beat an offer like that so I had everything to play for.

'Ladies' Final, Court No. 1,' announced the PA system. I froze. Court No. 1 was the only grass court on the complex and I'd never played on grass. I'd been pretty nervous already, now I was shattered.

The match was a bit of curate's egg. I won most of my service games, but too often found that the ball wasn't where I expected it to be; bounce and speed were totally different from that of the tarmac courts that were standard issue in the valley towns.

Eventually I lost, but I gave my opponent a good run for her money, and she had to play three sets to beat me.

I was disappointed but philosophical. I had been thrilled and quite surprised to survive the early rounds of the tournament, so reaching the Final ahead of all the smart outfits and arms full of racquets tuned to elegant style and regular coaching was quite a thrill.

The gang were eloquent in their congratulations; you'd think I'd just won Wimbledon not lost the Swansea tournament. In spite of my defeat, they were adamant that I'd beaten the odds anyway, so we still had a lavish fish and chip supper.

Mam had thought it was a bit daft going all the way to Swansea just to play tennis, but then as the whole world slipped into a higher faster gear with the arrival of peace, she found so much of life 'daft', 'real twp'.

My imminent departure for London and college life took precedence in her fuss and worry scale now. Why couldn't I go to Cardiff? Plenty of places, colleges and stuff there. I could come home on the bus every day. How did I know this London College Hostel place was up to her standard? She'd never seen it.

Dad said nothing, but kept bringing home things that would be useful – a bedside lamp, a large trunk, a coffee mug. These were all laid out in the front room as evidence to anyone who called that I had indeed 'passed for college' and would soon be leaving for an uncharted world with only Mam's trepidation to guide me.

Going on holiday with Trev and his family was a welcome relief. Family holidays up to this point mostly varied between a week in Herefordshire with Aunty Doll, and day trips to Barry or Porthcawl.

Cornwall had always fascinated me with its image of foamy seas, sands of deepest gold, wild heather headlands and its tales of pirates and pixies.

After months of preparation of good sensible shoes, books and stationery, there was a sudden whirl of full skirts, strappy sandals and swimsuits.

Mam thought Cornwall was somewhere near the moon to hear her talk. Well, nearly foreign wasn't it?

Trev's family car was big and roomy, having begun its life as a taxi cab, so there was sufficient, if not ample room for Trev and his parents, his gran and myself. Trev's dad had planned the journey carefully, co-ordinating distance, time and speed.

On any journey to the West Country at that time, there was the dreaded Exeter traffic jam to contend with. Dual carriageways, motorways, town by-passes were all dreams in the future, and on leaving Somerset, all roads converged on Exeter. The resulting jams of holiday traffic were of sufficient length in time and distance to warrant mention on the BBC news and even the Pathe Pictorial news feature that ran between films at the cinema.

Trev's dad had a cunning plan to beat the jam. We would leave home at night to arrive at the dreaded bottleneck at 3.00 am when everyone else would be asleep. This left Mam in a bit of a quandary. She was thrilled that she had a daughter going off on a 'paid for' holiday, not staying with relatives. She was delighted that she had a daughter going off on holiday by car, proof of which could be seen by all the neighbours, parked outside our house, door to door mind! But setting off 10 o'clock at night? Coming in I should be, not going out.

I was pretty pleased myself. No humping of cases up and down hill, no waiting for buses, possibly in heavy rain, no 'standing room only' on a packed train. The bucket seat behind Trev's dad was just about as luxurious as any travelling had ever been for me.

I didn't wallow in the luxury for long; I was asleep before we crossed the river Severn and only woke to a pale pearly sky and Trev's mam and dad arguing over the finer points of navigation to get through the streets of Newquay to our boarding house destination.

It didn't matter that my room was tiny. After each day of long endless beaches, whipped by hissing surf and studded with rocky outcrops like chunky jewellery, then tramping sweeping moorland and exploring tiny coves , sleep was not a problem. I took in every experience like a thirsty drunk at a frothy pint.

Then it was our last evening.

Trev and I took a fish and chip supper and wandered down to the little harbour. Fish had never tasted so good eaten with the tang of salt coming off the sea. The dark was warm, with patches of light and shadow reflected from a full lemon cheese moon.

It should have been so romantic, but more than anything I felt a deep sadness and tears spilled down my cheeks. I was bewildered too; how could I not feel anything but happy after such a wonderful holiday? It was just not logical, but emotional and instinctive. I was suddenly aware of a door closing in my life with so many things coming to an end. The regular pattern of family life with its visits and seasonal rituals would go on without me, and our little gang would be scattered through colleges and universities all over the country. No more weekly highlight of the Saturday night hops, and who would care about battling for top place in the league of valley tennis clubs? I was at that point where every part of my life seemed to have nothing but partings and endings.

Of course there was a new door in front of me which beckoned with great promises, but who really knew what lay beyond? I was only sure of one thing; it would take more than a tin of Welsh Cakes to sustain me down this new path.